DILEMMAS OF
WELFARE POLICY

Why Work Strategies
Haven't Worked

Mildred Rein

Library of Congress Cataloging in Publication Data
Rein, Mildred.
Dilemmas of Welfare Policy

Bibliography: p. 163-172
Includes index.
1. Public welfare—United States. 2. Welfare
recipients—Employment—United States. I. Title.
HV95.R44 1982 362.5'82'0973   82-3726
ISBN 0-03-056137-X   AACR2

Published in 1982 by Praeger Publishers
CBS Educational and Professional Publishing
a Division of CBS Inc.
521 Fifth Avenue, New York, New York 10175 U.S.A.

© 1982 by Praeger Publishers

3456789   052   98765432

Printed in the United States of America

To my children,
Glen and Lisa

Contents

LIST OF TABLES AND FIGURE

Introduction

In 1935, when Aid to Dependent Children (ADC) was added to the Social Security Act, it was envisioned as a residual category that would dwindle away with future comprehensive coverage under the social insurance provisions of the act. Within this framework, it was expected that the program would provide for a small and diminishing client body. ADC was also intended primarily for the children of widows; it was later that the children of divorced and separated parents and, even later, unmarried parents, were included. The purpose of the program was in fact to enable mothers who were clearly thought to be outside the labor force to stay at home and care for their children. Early studies of ADC indicate that the primary policy interest was in the welfare or progress of these fatherless children who, together with their widowed mothers, unequivocally comprised a segment of the "deserving poor." In fact, the progress made by children in recipient families was attributed to the beneficial effects of a stable income from ADC; continuous periods of assistance were therefore considered desirable.

This tidy conception of ADC as assistance for a small group of the deserving poor who would eventually be covered by social insurance proved inadequate to the experience that followed. In 1950, mothers of children were included in the grant, and in 1962, Aid to Dependent Children became Aid to Families with Dependent Children. Soon various extensions covered the incapacitated father, foster children, and the unemployed father—thus now directing benefits to the economic resources of the family and even to families with clearly employable male heads. At the same time, more women in the general population began to enter the labor force, tempering the norm, that mothers should be at home and not working.

The inclusion of these relatively small groups of eligibles, however, was not sufficient to account for the ever-increasing numbers of recipients. In 1940 the program gave benefits to only one million individuals; by 1960, three million. This was still no cause for alarm but in the late 1960s participation burgeoned, and by 1970 as many as nine million people were beneficiaries of AFDC grants, thus tripling in the 1960–70 decade. By 1975 there were over 11 million AFDC recipients and a sense of crisis had emerged. In addition, the composition of the caseload deviated drastically from the original conception that it was primarily widows and their children who were being provided for. In 1940 as much as 40 percent of the caseload was comprised of children with deceased fathers; by 1966, only 5 percent of AFDC children had fathers who were not alive, decreasing to 2.6 percent by 1977. Instead, the proportion of divorced, separated, deserted, and unmarried parents increased until in 1977 they represented over 80 percent of the families (the remainder were essentially the incapacitated and unemployed fathers).

Internal factors such as eligibility expansion and inclusion of employable males coupled with the external phenomenon of increased participation of women in the labor force veered the AFDC program away from its original model. Paradoxically, as people began to feel a growing sense of their right to assistance society called for restricted access to assistance rolls. Greatly increased costs and caseloads, in combination with a recipient population that appeared to have voluntarily chosen welfare over marriage, engendered the notion that these now "undeserving" clients should be constrained from receiving public assistance and should be instead exhorted to work.

In 1967 Congress made a major effort to encourage work for AFDC recipients via the 1967 amendments, which at the same time created a new focus on social services largely geared to reducing dependency, a disregard of the first $30 earned income and one-third thereafter, and the Work Incentive (WIN) program making mandatory the registration of every "appropriate" recipient for work and training.

In the mid-1970s the emergence of a fiscal crisis in state and federal funding capability further exacerbated discontent with the growth of the AFDC rolls. Studies during this period that showed participation rates of higher than 90 percent among eligibles documented the belief that the program was indeed oversaturated. After 1975, the caseload started to level off and even decline slightly, but 1980 saw what appeared to be the beginning of another resurgence. The Reagan administration, intent upon reversing this trend, proposed a major overhaul of funding and administration of the program whereby control of AFDC would revert entirely to the states and would be subsidized by federal block grants. This far-reaching reorganization would relieve the federal government of raising its share of payments to the states when caseloads and benefits increase, thus capping federal outlays. The expectation is that when left to their own financial and administrative devices, states would have the incentive and the freedom to contain welfare. Already legislated among a host of other reforms is a program of "workfare," wherein about 800,000 recipients will be compelled to work off some of their benefits in low-level public jobs. Even now, work as a means to welfare control persists and has been revived in its most extreme form.

In light of the history, purpose, and focus of the AFDC program, the aims of this book are to understand the meaning of the increase in recipients, to document the work and welfare patterns of recipients, and to assess the efficacy of the work strategies employed to reduce costs and caseloads. In its broader implications, this is a study of the major diversion of a social program from its original conception and intent, government and public response to this change, and how this response has been worked out in practice.

More specifically, we trace the development of a policy attempting to shift the major income source of welfare-risk families from welfare to work, and examine the actual income sources of a segment of this population to ascertain to what extent the policy perspective and the lives of these people are consistent.

To explore this question, the book is divided into two parts, the first of which deals with the derivations of work as a policy in response to the rise in welfare costs and caseloads, and evaluates the efficacy of the three strategies that emerged to promote work. Research questions to be asked in this section are:

1. Why did work become the containment mechanism and why in the form of these particular strategies?
2. To what extent were these policies successful in promoting work?
3. What were the forces that impinged upon their success or failure?

The data to be used here consist primarily of government reports and publications, as well as the relevant evaluative literature and other secondary sources.

Underlying the policy of work for AFDC recipients was the critical assumption that AFDC family heads (by far mostly mothers) are not essentially attached to the labor force, that only a small percentage of them work, and that welfare is the almost exclusive and constant source of income for these families. This view stems from the official biennial AFDC surveys which for the past two decades have reported that only from 14 to 16 percent of AFDC mothers have earnings, and that only a small fraction of case closings are for reasons of employment. Thus, work would be promoted through services, incentives, and requirements. However, the official surveys capture work among the recipient population at one point in time—during the month that the surveys are taken. Other analyses derived from yearly census data have shown much larger proportions of the actual and potential recipient population at work. In addition, qualitative studies which use field methods have observed that welfare-risk families living in the ghetto areas of large cities typically have many more sources of income than welfare and work and that they piece together an income that is complex, varied, and changing.

The second half of the book then attempts to evaluate the validity of the assumption underlying work as a public policy by determining to what extent work is a source of income, how important welfare and other income sources are, and how stable is the income package. Corollary research questions are: How do work and welfare and other income sources affect total income and well-being? How does the receipt and levels of work and welfare income affect each other and relate to other income sources? How does welfare status, marital status, and race affect total income, work, welfare, and other income sources? And, how do typical income packages interact with personal, family, and lifestyle characteristics?

To answer these questions, an analysis was undertaken of all of the income sources of a selected sample of 206 families. The raw data was retrieved from the Panel Study of Income Dynamics (PSID), an annual survey of 5000 families oversampled for low income, from 1968 to date. This is a national survey conducted at the Institute for Social Research at the University of Michigan, that collects information on income sources, personal and family characteristics, employment behavior, consumption patterns, etc. Our analysis is in two parts: a qualitative look at the PSID survey data on 30 families and a quantitative approach to the study of the 206 families. Ten years of interviews (from 1968 to 1977) are addressed in the first effort, while eight years of data (from 1970 through 1977) are utilized in the latter. Since the PSID survey deals with *yearly* income sources, it is assumed that a more accurate picture of income will be obtained than through a snapshot of income at one point in time. One limitation, however, must be noted: this data does not indicate what *part* of a year an income source was received, for example, how many months out of the year.

The sample that was chosen for this study from the PSID data was a group of 206 families who had the following characteristics: they had been on welfare in at least one of the 10 study years, they were female-headed in at least one year, they had children under 18 years of age in all of the years, and they lived 15 miles or under from the center of a city of 50,000 or more in one of twelve urbanized states. In short, this was a selection of ever-welfare, ever-female-headed families with children who lived in inner-city metropolitan areas.

This inner-city group was chosen for many reasons (to be discussed in Chapter 5) but primarily because it was felt that the "welfare problem" is seen by policy-makers essentially as an inner-city phenomenon where intransigent recipients choose welfare over work as a way of life. It is this segment of the welfare-risk population that implicitly, if not overtly, is the target of welfare policies that attempt to constrain the AFDC caseload.

The choice of ever-welfare, ever-female-headed families enabled the data to be dichotomized into 1) the years on welfare and the years not on welfare, and 2) those families that were female-headed all ten years and those who were female-headed in one or more years and married in one or more years, i.e. had changed their marital status in the ten year period. It was hypothesized that both welfare status and marital status would be decisive in the determination of the sources and levels of income for these families.

The data was further broken down and analyzed by race. Race plays a part in the receipt of welfare income. Fully 50 percent of AFDC families are Black, a proportion highly incongruent with the proportion of Blacks in the overall population. It has also been shown that Blacks and Whites have different employment patterns, and therefore work income. Finally, big inner-city areas are differentially populated by race with Blacks being more predominant. It was therefore of interest to analyze work and welfare and other income sources by race.

To effect the preceding objectives, the book was organized in the following ways: In chapter 1, we document the "welfare crisis," explicate the theories that account for the rise in AFDC costs and caseloads, and relate these interpretations to the mechanisms that government selected to promote work among recipients. Chapters 2, 3, and 4 analyze the origins, legislative history, implementation, and efficacy of the three work strategies: social services, work incentives, and work requirements. In chapters 5 and 6, the work and welfare patterns and other income sources are examined in an effort to ascertain the magnitude and frequency of these sources, the relationship between them, and the congruence between the actual income packages of this population and the government's efforts to promote work.

1
The Crisis in Welfare

The Aid to Dependent Children (ADC) program was established under the Social Security Act of 1935. Since its inception, ADC has undergone a major transformation in size, cost, and clientele. The act established two approaches to relieving economic want: contributory social insurance in which entitlement to benefits is based on an earned right related to past contributions, and public assistance that is distributed after a demonstrated test of need. Social insurance was initially offered only to the aged and the unemployed—the aged through a nationally-administered old-age insurance scheme, the unemployed through a federal system largely controlled by the states. In 1939 a major transformation in the philosophy of insurance was initiated with the recognition that equity (a close relationship between contribution and benefits) and adequacy (taking account of family need) conflicted. The conflict was resolved in favor of adequacy as the new legislation extended coverage to widows and dependent children. In 1959 the second major change occurred with the introduction of benefits for the permanently disabled.

Public assistance was conceived of as a transitional measure to be used until the social insurance program matured in adequacy of benefits and extensiveness of coverage. It was designed for those who had no viable connection to the labor market. The aged, blind, and dependent children were categories of persons for whom the states had already made provisions and were presumed to be outside the labor force. The act assumed an orderly world consisting of those who worked and those who were unable to work. By 1961, the first major assault on this assumption came with the introduction of a program to aid the long-term unemployed—Aid to Families with Dependent Children

1

(AFDC) for Unemployed Parents, known as AFDC-UP. There was still confidence that, in time, social insurance would displace public assistance, but by the 1970s new in-kind means-tested programs had been introduced to aid those with special needs for food, medical care, fuel, and other necessities. These new provisions challenged the principle of unrestricted cash grants embodied in the Social Security Act of 1935.

This conception of social security proved utterly inadequate to define the experience that followed. Public assistance was gradually extended to other groups such as the disabled and the medically indigent, sometimes paralleling, sometimes leading the development of social insurance. ADC was expanded to include parents of dependent children, foster children, children beyond age 18, incapacitated fathers, and, as we have seen, unemployed fathers. By 1962, ADC, a program founded to focus only on children, became AFDC, a program directed at the economic resources of the family. Not only was the scope of coverage extended but AFDC benefits levels steadily increased, making it possible for families with higher incomes to become eligible.

But as important as these comprehensive structural changes were, they did not account for the immense growth in the size of the AFDC program. As the program grew in size and cost, the clientele, which in the early years had comprised mainly the children of deceased parents, evolved into a program primarily for families with absent but living parents.

The foregoing changes in the nature of the AFDC program's size, cost, and clientele led in the mid-1960s to a sense of crisis. At the same time, the focus on families rather than on children and the inclusion of the able-bodied unemployed veered assistance philosophy toward family responsibility for the support of all needy children. The working poor came to be included in those receiving assistance, and work preparation, work incentives, and work requirements became a new theme for welfare policy. These convergent forces produced a public policy that in principle was committed to reducing the number of recipients of AFDC in the long run, even though in the short run it accepted the need to further augment the size and cost of the program.

MANIFESTATIONS OF THE CRISIS

The crisis in welfare was focused primarily on the growing size of the AFDC program. Growth was expected in the early years after the Depression and as a result of wars that left families fatherless; it was also understandable during recessions and at other times of high unemployment. But AFDC was conceived of as a residual and transitional expedient that eventually would dwindle in size with the expansion of non-means-tested provisions for the retired, disabled, widowed, and unemployed. Instead, the policy designed to resolve the income-maintenance problems of a small distinct group of economically vulnerable families exploded into a large and seemingly uncontained program.

The number of AFDC recipients was roughly one million in 1940, two million in 1950, three million in 1960, nine million in 1970, 10 million in 1971, and over 11 million in 1975.[1] Between 1960 and 1970, the size of the clientele tripled, and if the million a year increase in the caseload of the early 1970s had continued, by 1980 there would have been 19 million recipients or six times the number in 1960. These gross figures created a feeling of alarm. As it turned out, however, developments in the second half of the 1970s took a different turn. As shall be seen, the number of recipients levelled off in 1972, declined steadily from 1975 to 1979, but then increased again in 1980.

A closer look at the fluctuating numbers will provide a better understanding of these phenomena. Figure 1.1 summarizes the long-term annual trends by averaging the number of recipients during the months of June and December for each year, and shows that the time between the inception of the program in 1936 and 1980 can be broken up into five distinct periods. From 1936 to 1943 (period 1) there was a dramatic rise and then a fall to a point about midway between the floor and the peak of that rise. Between 1943 and 1953 (period 2) an almost identical pattern is evident. We note that the sharp reductions in the number of recipients in both periods came toward the end of both World War II and the Korean War. From 1953 to 1966 (period 3) the pattern changed to one of gradual and steady increase. Although there were variations within this period, the overall growth was 6.3 percent per annum.

The fourth period, from 1966 to 1972, marks the "welfare crisis," with the average annual increase as high as 18.2 percent. Had the same yearly expansion taken place in period 4 as in period 3, the overall per annum increment for both periods would have been only 6.8 percent; but the sharp climb in period 4 is actually three times this amount. The Vietnam War, a significant event of this time, did not reduce the number of AFDC recipients as earlier wars appeared to have done in their time. Nor did fluctuations of the economy seem to affect the AFDC rolls. From 1966 to 1969 the unemployment rate was under 4 percent, lower than it had been since 1953; it was not until 1971 that it reached a high of 5.9 percent. It was, therefore, not only the rise in absolute numbers that created a sense of an AFDC crisis but also the seeming irrationality of the pattern of sudden rise. While unemployment levels declined from 1953 to 1966 there was a steady rise in the welfare rates.

Figure 1.1.
Number of AFDC Recipients, June and December, 1936–80

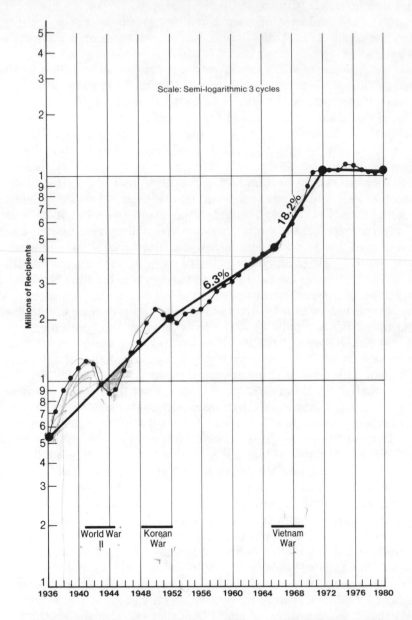

Source: Department of Health, Education and Welfare, SRS, NCSS, *Trend Report: Graphic Presentation of Public Assistance and Related Data*, 1971, p. 3; Department of Health and Human Services, SSA, *Public Assistance Statistics*, June and December, 1972 through 1980.

In the two previous periods an increase in economic prosperity had reduced welfare rolls. When the actual sharp rise in recipients came after 1966, the climate was fertile for alarm.

The fifth and last period (1972 to 1980) may best be characterized as one of levelling. The number of AFDC recipients began to fluctuate, decreasing in 1973, rising again slightly when it reached its highest point in the winter of 1975; thereafter it declined steadily until 1979.[2] But in 1980 the rolls started to increase again. In December 1980 the caseload in terms of recipients was 4.2 percent higher than in the same month a year earlier. Nevertheless the 1980 level was about the same as in the peak year 1975.[3] The decline between 1975 and 1979 was consistent with a drop in the unemployment rate from 8.7 percent to 5.9 percent in these years, and the rise in 1980 also paralleled a rise in the unemployment rate to 7.2 in 1980.[4] In this last period, then, fluctuations in the AFDC caseload appear to be related to general economic conditions, in contrast to the crisis period where no such link was visible.

Regardless of trends before and after, the period from 1966 to 1972 saw the greatest increase in the AFDC caseload and the most heightened belief in the presence of a welfare crisis. It must be noted, however, that the sense of alarm preceded this period as the rolls were already rising substantially, and continued later in spite of levelling off and decline. The following discussion will focus on the actual crisis period, although events in other years will be noted where appropriate.

The rise in numbers of AFDC recipients can be compared with the rise in recipients of other public assistance programs. A review of all five programs—Old Age Assistance (OAA), Aid to the Blind (AB), Aid to the Permanently and Totally Disabled (APTD) (these three retitled Supplementary Security Income (SSI) in 1974), General Assistance (GA), and AFDC, reveals that while there were parallel increases in the size of the first four programs, these increases did not approach the rise in AFDC. In 1950 AFDC recipients represented 36 percent of all recipients combined; in 1960, 43 percent; in 1970, 69 percent; and in 1971 as much as 72 percent.[5] But in the levelling period the pattern of AFDC dominance was weakened. By January 1980, AFDC recipients as a proportion of all cash assistance recipients decreased to 67 percent.[6]

Another measure of the magnitude of the problem is evident by looking at the recipients of these programs as a proportion of the total population. In 1971 there were 9.7 recipients per 1,000 persons on OAA, 5.5 recipients on AB and APTD, 4.7 on GA and as many as 51 recipients per 1,000 persons in the population on AFDC.[7] These figures for AFDC become even more dramatic when trends are examined and analysis is restricted to the child population. In 1950, 34 children per 1,000 of the child population were in the AFDC program; by 1970, this ratio had increased to 85 per 1,000.[8]

But size as reflected in the number of recipients was not the only source of anxiety for analysts of the crisis. The cost of the AFDC program was also an issue.* From 1950 to 1960 cash payments to recipients climbed gradually from $50 million to $1 billion. Between 1960 and 1970, however, the figure rose almost fivefold to just under $5 billion. Following the pattern of the rise in recipients, in 1971 payments rose another $1.4 billion and in 1972 another $706 million to reach the impressive sum of almost $7 billion. And in addition to cash payments there were funds for administration, medical assistance, and social services. By 1978, $10.7 billion were expended for cash payments to AFDC recipients.[9]

The cost of all public assistance programs together (including AFDC) also rose, again not as fast as AFDC and largely due to AFDC. From 1950 to 1960, cash payments to all recipients increased from $2.4 billion to $3.3 billion, but from 1960 to 1970 they almost tripled to $8.8 billion in 1970. In 1971 cash payments were $10.8 billion and by 1972 over $11 billion.† The proportionate share of AFDC payments rose from 3 percent to 31 percent between 1950 and 1960, to 55 percent in 1970 and to over two-thirds in 1972 and 1973.[10] In the fifth, levelling off, period, a major change in policy occurred. In 1974, programs for the aged, disabled, and blind were consolidated into SSI, a new federally-administered and financed program. When SSI was added to AFDC and GA, AFDC as a proportion of total welfare costs declined to 57 percent and remained at this level from 1974 to 1978.[11]

The rise in the size and cost of the AFDC program was impressive enough, but what appeared to be equally significant was the changing composition of the caseload and the nature of its transformation. At its inception in 1935 ADC had been conceived of as a program primarily for the children of widows. This evolved to include other categories of fatherless children such as those of the divorced, the separated, and the unmarried, until by 1950 families headed by widows comprised only 18 percent of the caseload. By 1961 the proportion of widowed families had dwindled to 6.8 percent, by 1967, 5.5 percent, by 1971, 4.3 percent, and by 1977, 2.6 percent.[12] Conversely, families with divorced, separated, deserted, and unmarried mothers grew. In 1950, 37 percent of the cases were in this category, but by 1961 the proportion had risen to 57 percent. In 1967, 70 percent were in this category and by 1971, almost

---

*If these figures are converted to constant 1967 dollars, the increase in expenditures from 1960 ($1.1 billion) to 1978 ($5.5 billion) is fivefold rather than elevenfold as when viewed in current dollars.

†If these figures are converted to constant 1967 dollars, the increase in expenditures from 1950 ($3.3 billion) to 1972 ($8.8 billion) is 2.6 times rather than 4.5 times as large.

73 percent of AFDC family heads were either divorced, separated, deserted, or unmarried; by 1977, the proportion had risen to 81 percent.[13]

Rapid and huge increases in the size and cost of the AFDC program and significant changes in its caseload in the 1960s created a sense of crisis among public assistance administrators, in federal, state, and local legislatures, and in the public mind. The ever-increasing size gave rise to the fear that endless numbers of recipients, including new groups such as the working poor, would enter the program. The concern was that those who were working at low wages would stop working and instead derive their income from AFDC. At the extreme, it was believed that if carried far enough, this would decimate the labor supply and erode the work ethic. The cost of the program would bankrupt state and local treasuries, especially in the large western and northeastern center-cities where most AFDC recipients lived.[14] The growth in broken families promoted fears that if such "irresponsible" behavior were rewarded by access to unearned income, it might eventually weaken the family as an institution.

The welfare crisis was seen by authorities as a financial, cultural, and political problem. The solution to the problem came out of an effort to contain the AFDC caseload's growth in size and cost, and evolved into a focus on *work* for AFDC family heads, who were mostly mothers. Work became the panacea as other more stringent solutions, such as eligibility restriction, were not feasible in the still liberal welfare climate of the mid-1960s. But the concept of work for the female heads of families with children met with resistance in some quarters where it was thought that these children needed their mother's care in the home. However, as more and more non-welfare mothers entered the labor force, it became clear that allowing women on welfare to stay at home would violate the principle of equity. While in AFDC's early years mothers were expected not to work, in order to protect the best interests of the children, caseload growth and demographic changes in the composition of the labor force resulted in a revision of this normative view. It was now expected that work would take the place of welfare and thus decrease the size and cost of the AFDC program.

Governmental efforts to institute work for family heads incorporated three strategies: social services, work incentives, and work requirements. These methods found their impetus and justification in the varying theories that had emerged to explain the rise in welfare costs and caseloads. Martin Rein has compiled a typology of interpretations of the reasons for the expansion of AFDC, which will be used below as a basis for our analysis of the strategies selected to implement work.[15]

EXPLANATIONS OF THE CRISIS

The first theory posed to explain the welfare rise is the weakening of family ties. This thesis begins with the disorganization of the family, especially the black family. The male head, ousted from the labor market, deserts his wife and children, leaving them to the beneficence of the welfare system. Such desertions can be real or pretended ("paper desertions") but in either case, they add to the welfare rolls. The increasing rates of separation and unmarried parenthood as reasons for the deprivation of children's support in the AFDC caseload support this formulation. In addition, only about half of the states have AFDC-UP programs; and GA provisions that include able-bodied males are not prevalent. Both AFDC-UP and GA have restrictive eligibility rules and strong work requirements, making basic AFDC an easier alternative. However, whether negatively or positively, the theory maintains that the welfare system plays a critical role in the support of the family disorganization phenomenon.

The AFDC program takes responsibility away from the father by expanding the choices open to the mother. Several studies have documented the relationship between the increase in female-headed families and increases in the AFDC caseload. Proponents of this view attribute the complicity of welfare to administrative laxity and to "a liberal philosophy of entitlement combined with adequate benefit levels."[16] This explanation, then, proposes that the essential reason for the growth of the AFDC program was the disorganization of the family, brought about mainly by economic circumstances and fostered by the welfare system itself.

Another suggested cause of the welfare crisis is the maldistribution of income. The earnings of low-wage workers are often insufficient to meet the needs of families with children. When this situation is compounded by equally or more remunerative welfare benefits, such families become eligible for AFDC. This formulation holds that the discrepancy between wages and benefits increased in the mid-1960s and early 1970s as benefits expanded faster than wages. Such relatively high welfare payments had a dual effect in enlarging the caseload; due to higher grant levels, more families became eligible, and welfare became more desirable than work.

AFDC benefits rose substantially between 1965 and 1972 and continued to rise thereafter. In 1965 the average monthly payment per recipient was $33; in 1972 it was $53.[17] Although later benefit rises were mitigated by inflation, in the years cited above this was not a significant factor. In some states family benefits exceeded the poverty line. In fiscal 1973, 24 percent of all AFDC recipients across the nation were not "in poverty."[18] While benefits have risen absolutely, they have also expanded relative to earnings. A comparison of average earnings of all private employees and the average monthly payment per AFDC recipient from 1963 to 1971 shows that earnings increased by only 42 percent while the AFDC payment increased by 67 percent.[19] In 1974, 61 percent of all AFDC recipients lived in the 28 states where the benefit for a family of four persons exceeded the net pay from a minimum wage job.[20]

It is this disparity between the benefits of welfare and the remuneration of work that was a major factor in the rise in AFDC, according to the maldistribution of income thesis. An empirical analysis of a benefit increase in New York City makes this process clear. In 1968, benefits were increased there by 7 percent—an amount yielding about $250 per year for a four-person family. Gordon notes that "the slight dollar increase immediately causes an increase of 300,000 in the number of eligibles . . . and after the August increase, close to half of the city's minority population lived in families that were eligible to receive welfare payments. . . . Many of these families naturally decided to claim what the state had to offer."[21]

Still another effort to interpret the growth in the AFDC program is the theory of civil disorder that emerged from the controversial Piven and Cloward book *Regulating the Poor*.[22] "They argue that relief expands to cope with disorder and contracts when stability is restored. A market system is characteristically plagued by periods of depression or stages of modernization and the net effect of both of these processes is to displace large numbers of individuals from employment."[23] The socializing effects of work are then lost and family obligations become weaker. Relief is then offered by government as a way of both quieting ("cooling out") unrest and as a substitute for the usual regulatory mechanisms of work and family.

Instability in the early- and mid-1960s resulted in an expansion of access to the welfare system, in more liberal eligibility policies, and in higher benefits. Given this opportunity, families who could gain little reward from labor-force participation elected instead to accept welfare largesse. This process involved two sets of actors—poor families, and welfare managers and policy makers, the latter responding to the threat of civil disorder by providing easy access and generous assistance conditions that encouraged participation.

Some empirical evidence gives credence to the potential effect of these program parameters on participation. Boland, using national data, estimates that "while the eligible pool increased by 24 percent between 1967 and 1970, the caseload doubled, suggesting that the rate of participation increased substantially. . . . For the female-headed portion of the caseload, participation increased from 63 percent to 91 percent."[24] Jencks also points out that although the number of female-headed families had grown from 4.4 million in 1960 to 5.4 million in 1970, the number of AFDC families rose from 0.7 million to 2.3 million in the same period.[25] The rate of participation, then, was 18 percent in 1960 and as high as 41 percent in 1970. (This estimate takes into account *all* such families and not only those who were eligible, as does Boland's.)

While the maldistribution of income hypothesis attributes the rise to an increased pool of eligibles, the supposition that civil disorder was responsible for the welfare rise assumes that higher participation rates were the decisive factor. The next section will explain the relationship between the Rein typology of interpretations of the welfare rise and the strategies that were employed to promote work.

STRATEGIES TO PROMOTE WORK

The strategies instituted by government to cultivate work among AFDC recipients had a direct though not necessarily overt connection to the theories that were being advanced to explain the welfare crisis. In the family disorganization thesis, it is assumed that an individual willfully deconstitutes his family unit so as to become eligible for welfare benefits. While this may be a rational choice based on economic circumstances, it nevertheless results in pathological anti-social behavior and a debilitated family structure.

This, then, was essentially a sociological interpretation of the major causes associated with the rise in welfare. As such, social remedies were needed to ameliorate the problem. As will be seen in the next chapter, social services were legislated in 1962 in an attempt to rehabilitate and strengthen the family unit. It was the social services establishment, largely staffed by members of the social work profession, that was successful in introducing services into the realm of federal programs. Although in 1967 Congress reoriented social services in order to better encourage work, this interest group persisted in maintaining the strengthening of the family as a primary goal. When the focus on work could no longer be avoided, the child care service was proffered as a link between rehabilitative social services and provision of services as a work strategy. Today, child care remains the largest and most costly of all the social services available to AFDC families.

It is clear that social services policy designed to encourage work derived from the apparent weakening of family ties. The solution, therefore, was to strengthen the family through rehabilitative services. These services eventually became linked to more clearly work-oriented services such as child care and work training. Child care, however, continued to be geared primarily to efforts to reconstruct the AFDC family, with much less emphasis on its function as a work-enabling social service.

The maldistribution of income concept offers an economic explanation for the expansion of the AFDC program. When welfare benefits outstripped wages, work was forsaken and welfare became the better alternative. The challenge, then, was to make work worthwhile without lowering benefits. Economists interested in social welfare were concerned with questions of income distribution. They were convinced that the route out of poverty was through work, and they sought ways to make work more attractive. They were concerned with issues of equity, as well, that is, that those that worked while on welfare should receive compensation just as workers outside the welfare system did. Thus, they fashioned the idea of work incentives. Although the work incentive strategy was the basis for the negative income tax proposals in the late 1960s and throughout the 1970s, it had already taken root in the "thirty and one-third" earnings exemption legislated for the AFDC program in 1967. The principle of partial earnings retention became a major aspect of the effort to promote work in AFDC.

The notion that it was the threat of civil disorder that created the rise in the AFDC caseload is a political view. Such a threat creates a responsive welfare system where access to welfare is expanded and conditions for those on welfare are improved. Since the predominant motive of welfare reform is considered to be social control designed to preserve the marginal position of the poor, the poor, it is suggested, are justified in taking advantage of easy access and in pressing for special privileges. As political unrest diminishes and stability returns, the welfare administration resumes tightened eligibility procedures, depletes access, and institutes work requirements.

The first work requirements for AFDC mothers were legislated in the 1967 amendments, which established the Work Incentive program (WIN). However, as will be seen in Chapter 4, in practice these requirements were not applied to female family heads, whose participation was essentially voluntary. Even male heads of AFDC families received very few sanctions for noncompliance, although their involvement in the program was clearly mandatory according to the amendments. Since only a small proportion of the caseload became enrolled in WIN, the early program was more a registration requirement than a work requirement. Subsequent legislative efforts attempted to institute more

rigorous participation policies, but it was not until the Omnibus Reconciliation Act of 1981 that stringent work requirements (at least in principle) became a reality.

The history of work requirements as a means to compel work effort
in AFDC did appear to relate to the civil disorder theory. As a result of
liberalized welfare policies in the mid-1960s and early 1970s, some
welfare managers and conservative politicians saw the welfare problem
in terms of administrative flaws that encouraged easy access, laxity,
and fraud. Early on, these groups were instrumental in establishing
work requirements, but since political unrest was still in the air these
requirements were never enforced. Once it was seen that political
stability had been achieved, the Reagan administration radically expanded such requirements.

The ensuing chapters will discuss the three work strategies—social
services, work incentives, and work requirements. Work and welfare
patterns of recipients will then be examined and related to these governmental efforts to induce work among AFDC family heads. The concluding chapter summarizes these findings and offers an alternative to
the present policies to promote work.

NOTES

1. U.S. Department of Health and Human Services, Social Security Administration,
Social Security Bulletin (Annual Statistical Supplement, 1977–79, September 1980),
p. 248.

2. *Social Security Bulletin*, December 1980, p. 59.

3. U.S. Department of Health and Human Services, Social Security Administration,
Public Assistance Statistics December 1980, p. 14.

4. U.S. Department of Health and Human Services, Social Security Administration,
Social Security Bulletin 44, no. 12 (December 1981): 61.

5. U.S. Department of Health, Education and Welfare, Social and Rehabilitation Service, *Trend Report: Graphic Presentation of Public Assistance and Related Data* (1971),
p. 3.

6. *Social Security Bulletin*, December 1981, pp. 43, 49.

7. *Trend Report*, p. 19.

8. Russel B. Long, *The Welfare Mess: A Scandal of Illegitimacy and Desertion*, U.S.
Senate, Committee on Finance, December 14, 1971, pp. 12, 13.

9. *Social Security Bulletin*, September 1980, p. 248.

10. *Social Security Bulletin*, December 1981, p. 50.

11. *Social Security Bulletin*, September 1980, pp. 218, 248, 250.

12. David B. Eppley, "Decline in the Number of AFDC Orphans: 1935–1966," *Welfare
in Review* (September–November 1968), pp. 1–7; U.S. Department of Health, Education
and Welfare, SRS, NCCS, *Findings of the 1967 AFDC Study*, Part I: "Demographic and
Program Characteristics," Table 22; U.S. Department of Health, Education and Welfare,
SRS, NCSS, *Findings of the 1971 AFDC Study*, Part I: "Demographic and Program Charac-

teristics," Table 15; U.S. Department of Health and Human Services, SSA, ORS, *1977 Recipient Characteristics Study*, Part 1: "Demographic and Program Statistics," p. 51.

13. Gordon W. Blackwell and Raymond F. Gould, *Future Citizens All* (Chicago: American Public Welfare Association, 1952), p. 21; U.S. Department of Health, Education and Welfare, Welfare Administration, *Characteristics of Families Receiving Aid to Families with Dependent Children, November–December 1961*, Table 33; *Findings of the 1967 AFDC Study*, Table 22; *Findings of the 1971 AFDC Study*, Table 15; *1977 Recipient Characteristics Study*, p. 51.

14. Barbara Boland, "Participation in the Aid to Families with Dependent Children Program," *The Family Poverty and Welfare Programs: Factors Influencing Family Stability, Studies in Public Welfare*, Paper No. 12, Joint Economic Committee, U.S. Congress, 1973, p. 153. Boland documents that in both 1967 and 1970 female-headed families living in northeastern and western central cities have had higher AFDC participation rates than other groups.

15. Martin Rein, "The Welfare Crisis" in *Inequality and Justice*, ed. Lee Rainwater (Chicago: Aldine, 1974), pp. 89–102.

16. Rein, "The Welfare Crisis," p. 95.

17. *Economic Report of the President, 1979* (Washington, D.C.: Government Printing Office, 1979), p. 169.

18. *Economic Report of the President*, p. 168.

19. Sar A. Levitan, Martin Rein, and David Marwick, *Work and Welfare Go Together* (Baltimore: Johns Hopkins University Press, 1972), p. 14.

20. Vee Burke and Alair A. Townsend, "Public Welfare and Work Incentives: Theory and Practice," *Studies in Public Welfare*, Paper No. 14, Joint Economic Committee, U.S. Congress, 1974, p. 13.

21. David M. Gordon, "Income and Welfare in New York City," *The Public Interest*, no. 16 (Summer 1969), p. 81.

22. Frances Fox Piven and Richard C. Cloward, *Regulating the Poor: The Functions of Public Welfare* (New York: Pantheon, 1971).

23. Rein, "The Welfare Crisis," p. 97.

24. Boland, "Participation in the AFDC Program," p. 139.

25. Christopher Jencks, "Alternatives to Welfare," *Working Papers for a New Society* 1, no. 4 (Winter 1974): 159.

2

Work Through Social Services

This chapter* will discuss provision of social services as a work strategy, giving attention to the services amendments to the Social Security Act, the guidelines that emanated from them, and the resulting practice. Although self-support has been an acknowledged goal in all the amendments, it has been emphasized in varying degrees at different times. From 1956 to 1967 the competing goal of "strengthening family life" gave primary importance to rehabilitating the AFDC family, a process that, it was hoped, would lead to economic independence. With the passage of the 1967 amendments, work for family heads became a dominant objective to be achieved by work-related social services. This aim, however, was deflected by groups outside of the federal welfare administration who were more interested in fiscal solvency and a dispersion of social services to higher income families. Finally, the year 1974 saw a return of social services purposes to the rehabilitative function and an attrition of the self-support goal.

THE 1962 AMENDMENTS: REHABILITATION

Aside from the problems of increased size and cost of the program, AFDC families were exhibiting "problem behavior." Desertion, child neglect, and delinquency were the concerns of the day and could be traced in preponderance to those families in the program. It was discovered in 1951 that a small proportion of the poor were absorbing a

---

*This is an updated and revised version of "Social Services as a Work Strategy" which appeared in *Social Service Review* 49, no. 4 (December 1975).

large proportion of social welfare resources, and in professional jargon these became known as the multiproblem or "hard-to-reach" families. Urban anthropologists like Walter B. Miller were describing this population in terms of a "culture of poverty," a concept that was applied to the AFDC recipients. The professionals who were involved in the administration of the program were becoming open to charges of laxity and leniency.

In 1961 an ad hoc committee was formed consisting of two dozen professionals headed by Wilbur Cohen, Assistant Secretary of the Department of Health, Education and Welfare (HEW), to advise the administration on policy matters relating to public assistance. The committee's recommendations were heavily weighted in the direction of "services" for AFDC families, toward the goals of prevention and rehabilitation. Gilbert notes that "services, research and training were means of countering the assertion that fraud and laxity in public welfare stemmed from professional social work with the more realistic argument that they reflected insufficient professionalism."[1] The 1962 amendments, largely based on these recommendations, were proposed as a panacea for the rising rolls and the changing clientele of the AFDC program.

The main thrust of the 1962 amendments was services, and the purpose of these services as stated in the legislation was to "help maintain and strengthen family life and to help such parents or relatives to attain or retain capability for the maximum self-support and personal independence consistent with the maintenance of continuing parental care and protection." President Kennedy, when he signed the bill, said it was "to prevent or reduce dependency and to encourage self-care and self-support—to maintain family life where it is adequate and to restore it where it is deficient."[2] HEW Secretary Abraham Ribicoff pointed to the two objectives to which new welfare legislation must address itself: "eliminating whatever abuses have crept into these programs and developing more constructive approaches to get people off assistance and back into useful roles in society."[3] According to Lurie, "Congressional committees accepted the bill as a method of reducing welfare costs."[4]

Out of the melange of aims inherent in the amendments, two broad interests can be extracted: that of strengthening family life and that of moving recipients of AFDC toward self-support. The former was a response to the high incidence among AFDC clients of ineligibility for welfare, child neglect, delinquency, and desertion, and resulted in the professional solution of rehabilitation. The self-support feature was addressed to growing rolls and rising costs in an effort to reduce public dependency. Strengthening family life was directed toward the goal of changing the clientele—the caseload composition of the program—

while self-support was designed to reduce size and cost. Whether these two interests were compatible, and whether the services strategy could bridge the gap between them, was questionable.

In 1956, the 1935 Social Security Act had been amended to include the provision of services. The same purposes—"self-care, self-support and strengthening family life" as enacting the views of HEW and the profession of social work—were expressed, but, as noted by Gilbert, "The 1956 amendments had little effect on the rendering of services."[5] Services were left optional with the states and no financial incentive was given for the states to provide them, as they were "inserted" for purposes of federal reimbursement into the 50 percent matching formula accorded all other administrative activities.

Under the 1962 formula, the states would receive the standard 50 percent matching funds for providing certain services. Other so-called "prescribed services," if offered, would yield 75 percent reimbursement from the federal government. A 1964 HEW publication refers to federal policies that had emerged from the 1962 service amendments and defines the 50 percent services as: casework, community planning, group work, homemaker service, volunteer service, foster care, and training for self-support or self-care. Seventy-five percent services are defined by groups to be serviced: all families with adults with potential for self-support, all unmarried parents and their children with special problems, all families disrupted by desertion, all children in need of protection, and all children with special problems. The methodology for improving self-support potential is "casework services to assess capacity for and, if appropriate, promote self-support; to remove personal or family barriers to self-support and to encourage the adult to upgrade skills and to secure and maintain suitable employment; and the use of community resources for evaluation of employment potentials, vocational training, necessary medical services, security employment and for child care."[6] The report goes on to say that "casework, including full use of related community resources, and community planning are the only service methods that are required in carrying out the above services."[7]

The services legislated by the 1962 amendments were not implemented to any substantive degree. The HEW publication cited above, reviewing a 21-month period after the amendments became effective, points out that 18 states together had added only 50 full-time and 20 part-time staff members to carry out the service function. Seventeen states reported that they jointly had only 287 specialists devoting 50 percent of their time to social services.[8]

The 1967 national (HEW) AFDC statistics paint a somewhat more positive picture of services rendered. They show that as many as 80 per-

cent of all AFDC families had received at least one type of service. The
description of these services, however, modifies this optimistic estimate. "Health care" is defined as a social service provided to as many as
33 percent of recipient families, although it is not clear whether this
refers to medical efforts by the welfare agency or care through ordinary
free clinic service. Similarly, "protection of children" is a service that
was given to 11.5 percent of the families, but referral to child protective
agencies—ostensibly what is being considered here—had taken place in
welfare offices long before the "service orientation" instituted by the
1962 amendments. Other services that fall into the area of "strengthening family life" are loosely defined as "improved family functioning,"
25.4 percent; "maintaining the home," 17.5 percent; and "maintaining
or improving social relationships and participation in community life,"
8 percent. Self-support services, also not specified, were received by only
8.6 percent of all families.[9] It is difficult to see how these obscure
categories could be defined as specific services and how it could be
established that a service had been rendered by the welfare agency.

Gilbert gives the reasons why, in his view, services in AFDC never
quite became a reality: the 1962 amendments did not actually define
services, and neither was Congress able to specify them. The problem
of definition was left to the professionals. In the welfare agencies,
operational obstacles arose when it was not known whether to classify
recipients in terms of problems, methods, or services. The lack of standards by which to allocate, measure, and evaluate services created
problems. It was not clear how to match a professional activity
(casework) with the formal requirements of vast, bureaucratically-
oriented public assistance agencies. The professional explanation was
later expressed in terms of lack of sufficient professional staff to carry
out the service function.

If the dual intent of services was to strengthen family life and
reduce dependency, this was surely not carried out. The rate of illegitimacy in AFDC families rose after 1962: in 1961, 21.3 percent of
families included a father not married to the mother; in 1967, 28.4 percent.[10] The proportion of families with divorced, separated, or deserted
parents was 40.5 percent in 1961 and 45.3 percent in 1967.[11] Provision
of services did not appear to be an effective solution, at least to preventing family breakup. Neither was dependency reduced as the number of
recipients increased from over 3.5 million in 1961 to almost 5.0 million
in 1967.[12]

From 1967 on, it was acknowledged that services were "sold" to
Congress in 1962 as a means of reducing dependency. The promise and
the failure of services to do so may, in fact, have led to more stringent

measures taken later to effect this goal. The 1962 amendments legislated the first significant attempt to use services as a strategy for both changing the client body through strengthening family life and reducing the AFDC rolls by encouraging self-support. These were the beginnings of the focus on work as a remedy for the welfare crisis.

Despite the failure of 1962 social services to make an impact on the AFDC caseload, in 1967 Congress was still interested in the concept. But services now would have to be different from the preceding five years of "casework." For one thing, the goal of work for AFDC family heads became more explicit and was no longer couched in rehabilitative terms. The War on Poverty had made acceptable the idea that the poor would themselves benefit by becoming self-sufficient and also had a right to the opportunity to do so. Furthermore, job training and related services that had been offered by the Office of Economic Opportunity were conveniently conceptualized and were appropriate for welfare recipients. The question of which services to offer had already been answered. Services in public assistance were now to be concrete and work-oriented. Personal competence, the aim in 1962, became skills competence and was to lead less circuitously to work.

THE 1967 AMENDMENTS: WORK

The major vehicle for implementing work and training created by the 1967 amendments was the WIN program. This program made the involvement of certain employable family heads in work and training mandatory, but also allowed for voluntary enrollment. If an AFDC mother was selected for this program, she would, by law, have to be provided with free child care by the welfare agency. WIN was both a work requirement and a service but it was legislated under a different statute than the other social services. It had a different body of regulations, and a different matching formula. Subsequent amendments that altered the social services structure did not affect the WIN provisions. In addition to WIN, the 1967 amendments also legislated the "thirty-and-one-third" earnings exemption—a work incentive; a freeze on the number of new AFDC families with absent fathers allowed to enter the program—an effort to limit caseload growth (later repealed); and a permanent unemployed-parent segment—an attempt to keep families intact by removing the incentive to desertion. Clearly, Congress was determined to contain the growth of the AFDC caseload through work requirements, work incentives, social services, and other methods.

For social services, Congress reiterated the two goals of the 1962 amendments: self-support and the strengthening of the family. HEW's regulations to implement the services amendment required the states "to assist all appropriate persons to achieve employment and self-sufficiency, [to provide] child care services required to accept work or training, foster care services, family planning services, protective services, services related to health needs, and services to meet particular needs of families and children." The "particular needs" were defined as education, homemaking, housing, reuniting families, money management, consumer education, child rearing, education for family living, and protective and vendor payments. The states could provide optional services that would also be reimbursed. These were divided into two kinds: the full range of family services for the purpose of either strengthening the family or assisting a member to attain self-support; or selected services such as child care (whether or not needed for employment), emergency assistance, educational and training services (where there was no WIN program) and legal services.[13]

Aside from the wide range of services specified in the regulations, two very important stipulations were included, which later had extensive ramifications. The 1967 amendments (as had the 1962 amendments) called for services not only to public assistance clients but also to former and potential clients. The purpose of this as in 1962 was to carry out the broad goal of the prevention of dependency, and the regulations now defined "former" as welfare recipiency within the previous two years and "potential" as within the next five years. Eligibility for service was thus theoretically extendable to a large target population outside of welfare although it had not been used this way after the 1962 amendments. Another little-practiced feature of the 1962 amendments was also broadened in 1967—the purchase of services by the welfare agency from other agencies. While in 1962 this only allowed purchase from other public agencies, the 1967 amendments authorized purchase of services from private agencies or agents as well.

The "particular needs" and "full range" clauses of the regulations created a comprehensive array of specified services under which headings almost any service was federally reimbursable. Thus while congressional aims for social services inhered mainly in the area of work and the prevention of family breakup—both assumed to lead to the reduction of the welfare rolls—these aims were already diverted in the regulations that greatly broadened the scope of services. The broad scope of services was, moreover, matched by the vast numbers of possible recipients of such services as defined by the two- and five-year-eligibility requirements. The purchase of services from both public and private sources, as will be seen later, also served to curtail the primary intent of the 1967 amendments.

PRACTICE IN AFDC

But how did the intent to curb the growth of the AFDC caseload through social services fare in practice? To what extent were services work-related after 1967? The only comprehensive account of services was given in the national AFDC study that is periodically conducted by HEW, based on a sampling of the states' cases. The data are derived from caseworker reports that a service has been rendered, not from recipient statements that a service has been received. What is certain is that all these services were federally reimbursed. The 1971 AFDC study lists 30 services and indicates that in that year at least one service was provided in 81 percent of the families.[14] But these impressive figures need to be analyzed further to determine whether the given number of services were actually provided and how many of them were related to work. In order to do this, we have divided the 30 services into four categories: eligibility-related, concrete, competence-enhancing, and work-related.

Eligibility-related services are those necessary to carry out the income-maintenance function of the agency, such as "services to establish paternity of children" without which condition, in fact, eligibility for AFDC does not exist. Such procedures were not considered services until the 1967 services amendments took effect; the "service" designation stems both from the potential for federal reimbursement and the professional view of what constitutes a service. Handler summarizes Wisconsin's policy:

> . . . every aspect of AFDC administration can be considered a social service. The determination of eligibility and the administration of the budget . . . if done properly, may have a social service or rehabilitative value. . . . The administration of money payments is supposed to encourage home management and client responsibility.[15]

Concrete services such as child protective services, legal services, and homemaker services have no bearing on employment but are concerned with aspects of daily functioning. Competence-enhancing services are those that may help to strengthen family life, such as "family-planning information and counseling," "services related to parent-child relationships or other child-adjustment problems" and a host of others including only one relevant to employment: "counseling, guidance, or other diagnostic services related to employment." As casework services, these are open to the same charges as were the 1962 services: they are essentially unreportable and unable to be evaluated. Handler says of this kind of service that it is "in the main . . . little more than a relatively infrequent, pleasant chat, . . . qualitatively, the dominant characteristic of the service is one of minimum intervention."[16] There is no way of monitoring caseworker contacts with clients or their results in relation to an area such as employment.

Of the 30 listed services in the 1971 AFDC study only five are concrete and directly work-related. These are vocational rehabilitation, vocational education, day care, preschool education, and referral for employment or work training. Only 8 percent of the families received vocational rehabilitation, 8 percent vocational education, 7 percent day care, 7 percent preschool education, and 24 percent referral for employment or work training.

Given the limitations of this official account of services to AFDC families in 1971, we can only elicit some impressions. First, many of the services that are listed may not be services at all; these are the eligibility-related services. The second group of services that is questionable are those that deal with competence-enhancement, as it is difficult to say whether they were actually given in the context of the caseworker-client relationship. As for services that are concrete and directly work-related, it is not possible to know how many families actually received such services. It is clear that, aside from the 24 percent of families that received "referral for employment or work-training" (which is largely the WIN category), the proportion that received work-related services as compared with those who received the host of services not related to work is extremely small.[17]

Another estimate of the extent to which services were work-related can be made by looking at social services expenditures. A study requested by and prepared for HEW by an independent research firm lists 22 services under Title IV-A comprising federal, state, and local expenditures. Total expenditures in 1971 were $1.7 billion for all services. Only three of the 22 services listed were work-related: child care, WIN employment and training, and employment and training (non-WIN). WIN employment and training accounted for only 9 percent of the total expenditure, employment and training only 4 percent; child care took a large 29 percent.[18] This figure, however, is misleading insofar as AFDC families are concerned. Title IV-A covered both welfare recipients and former and potential welfare recipients, and there is no way of separating AFDC families. As will be clarified later, a large proportion of the 29 percent expended for child care was for child care services to non-welfare families. Taking this into account, we are again left with the conclusion that only a small part of social services expenditures were for work-related services.

Even where work-related services were given in AFDC, were they, in fact, related to work? Let us examine the work-related service given to the largest proportion of AFDC families and accounting for the largest such expenditure—child care. When day care and pre-school education are combined, we note that 308,600 families received this service in 1971.[19] Did those at work receive this service, which was intended to facilitate employment for the AFDC mother? In 1971 there were 510,000 AFDC families where the mother was either working, enrolled in a work-training program, or awaiting enrollment in WIN. But only 18 percent of full-time employed and 13 percent of part-time employed mother families received the child care service.* Being enrolled in a training program was more fortuitous (no doubt due to the requirement that WIN mothers must be given child care). Forty-one percent of these families got child care as did 19 percent of mothers awaiting enrollment.[20]

Where then did the bulk of these services go if not to the working mothers? The composition of the recipient group is revealing. Only 36 percent of the families receiving child care as a service contained mothers who were working, training, or awaiting training. The balance of these families—a startling 64 percent—were in other categories. The mother was incapacitated in 7 percent of families, had no suitable skills in 5 percent, was actively seeking work in 7 percent, was not actively seeking work in 8 percent (with more *not* actively seeking work), and was "needed in the home as a homemaker" in the largest group—33 percent of the families. In all, 308,600 families received the child care service but only 111,106 of them had mothers who were at work or in WIN. The overlap between this group and the 510,000 mothers in a work-related status is minimal.[21] The same pattern held true in 1973. In that year, of 668,523 families where the mother was "away from home on a recurrent basis" only 124,291 received vendor payments for child care.[22] That is, only 18 percent of these mothers (546,793 of whom were actually at work or in WIN) received child care as a social service.[23] Conversely, while 281,361 families had the child care service, only 44 percent of these mothers were engaged in work or training.[24] The bulk of this service in both years went to families where the mother was not work-oriented.

The provision of child care services for purposes other than the

---

*In 1971 an additional 142,800 families had the cost of child care deducted from income from work before welfare eligibility was determined, and received "free" child care this way. But even when these are added to the 111,106 families who received child care as a service, only half of the 510,000 work-oriented mother families were covered. In 1973, too, when the 148,645 families with income disregards for child care are combined with the 124,291 that got the child care service, only half of the working and training mother families were provided for. (*Findings of the 1971 AFDC Study*, Table 73, and *Findings of the 1973 AFDC Study, Part II*, Table 43.)

employment or training of the mother was legitimized under the "optional" clause of the HEW regulations (the same regulations made child care mandatory for working or training mothers). The extent to which this residual child care category assumed such importance in practice is startling. From the beginning, there has been a tension between the child-minding and the developmental functions of child care, especially in formalized day care. In the mid-1960s the War on Poverty focused on the right of the poor to services, on day care as a means by which poor children could be taught to overcome their cultural disadvantages, and on the benefits that would accrue to society as a result of such changes. This ideology coincided with professional interests in day care as part of a comprehensive package of services to a family, designed for rehabilitation.

Although Congress intended child care in 1967 to be primarily for the purpose of enabling AFDC mothers to work, both day care theory and facilities by that time had already been heavily influenced by the developmental ideology. HEW itself housed proponents of this point of view and carried on the 1962 rehabilitation function of social services despite the 1967 emphasis on services as a means to promote employment. A report prepared for the Department of Labor (DOL) discusses the high standards for day care centers that the federal government required for funding:

> Perhaps part of the problem can be attributed to the great interest in the theory of day care and the lack of interest in the nuts and bolts of actually getting care to the working mother so that she can use it. The Federal Interagency Day Care Standards are a good illustration of this problem. They emphasize "developmental" issues to such a degree that they have proved costly and impractical for large scale adoption of day care for children of manpower trainees.[25]

In this vein, day care centers serving welfare and other poor families were geared to the developmental function. The Westinghouse-Westat Day Care study divided day care centers into three types: custodial, educational, and developmental. This study discovered that the developmental type, which had the lowest number of children per staff person, the most highly trained professional staff, and offered the most comprehensive list of family services, was also the type that was most funded by government money and served the highest percent of families with low income, many of which were on welfare.[26] A Brookings Institution publication summarizes the state of affairs: "To a significant extent, a two-class system has evolved in day care, with a small proportion of the poor getting more comprehensive and costly care in subsidized day care centers than is available to the non-poor in unsubsidized centers."[27] The developmental focus of these subsidized day care centers which, in fact, did service AFDC mothers, may account largely for the bulk of child care services in AFDC going to nonworking mothers.

FORMER AND POTENTIAL AFDC RECIPIENTS

But the fact that within AFDC most child services went to families with nonworking and nontraining mothers is not the whole story of the allocation of child care services under the AFDC title of the Social Security Act. HEW, embarrassed and puzzled over AFDC recipient statistics that showed child care being used largely as a nonwork-related service, conducted its own private survey of the states early in 1973. According to some HEW officials the survey found that 70 percent of child-care services under Title IV-A went to work-related families (this contrasts with the 1971 AFDC study indicating that this proportion was used by nonwork-related families).

The discrepancy may be explained by the number of "former and potential" recipients of AFDC social services who were, in fact, not recipients of AFDC cash benefits. In one official's view, former and potentials may have accounted for from 40 to 60 percent of the families receiving child care services. However, this represents only a possible range and not an exact figure. It is not clear how many services recipients were indeed not welfare recipients. In this regard, Lurie notes that "published data do not permit an estimate of the extent to which expenditures on services are being used to help people who are not on welfare, but it may have become considerable in the past few years."[28]

National figures are not available but a General Accounting Office (GAO) 1971 survey of Title IV-A funded day care centers in Pennsylvania and California found that out of a sample of 331 families, 149 were assistance recipient families while as many as 182 were not.[29] Using income as an indicator of welfare status may shed further light. A Joint Economic Committee report comments on who was eligible for day care services in New York City in centers largely funded by Title IV-A funds: ". . . higher income families . . . are receiving a substantial subsidy and can continue to receive it no matter how high their income goes."[30] Families with annual incomes of $10,500 or more were eligible and were, of course, not on AFDC.

The services provision for former and potential AFDC recipients was in the interest of preventing dependency. It is relevant therefore to ask whether these non-welfare families receiving subsidized day care were, in fact, at work. What evidence there is seems to show that child care for these families, too, was not heavily work-related. As noted, the day care centers that were publicly funded were developmentally and not custodially focused. The Joint Economic Committee report claims that "the New York City program has moved towards a concept of universal day care providing early childhood development programs."[31]

Although state and national figures are not available, the GAO study shows that out of 7,200 children receiving Title IV-A child care services in Pennsylvania, 56 percent had parents who were at work or in training, while 44 percent "were enrolled solely to obtain social or educational benefits."[32] The report concludes that "the low use of services by Work Incentive Program participants and the relatively large number of program enrollees whose parents were not working or training raise serious questions as to whether child care services achieve the primary objective of the program, to help welfare families become self-sufficient."[33] Furthermore, both California and Pennsylvania state plans did "not provide for a systematic method of meeting the need for services so that the needs of public assistance recipients who are working or training are given priority."[34] It would appear, then, that the practice of social services after the 1967 amendments was not primarily work-oriented in AFDC, and was substantially geared to nonwelfare recipients, at least in child care, a high proportion of whom did not use the service for work-related purposes.

THE SERVICES EXPLOSION

From 1967 onward, federal grants to the states for social services increased gradually from $282 million in that year to $741 million in 1971. These figures include services in all the public assistance programs under the Social Security Act. From fiscal year 1971 to fiscal year 1972 this cumulative federal grant rose to $1.6 billion, more than doubling.[35] In the Title IV-A component alone in 1972 all sources (federal, state, and local) spent $1.8 billion or 123 percent more than was spent in 1971.[36] But these huge increases did not signify corollary increases in services. The HEW-commissioned study of the "Cost Analysis of Social Services, Fiscal Year 1972" discovered that the greatest part of the increase was due to the practice of purchase from both private and public agencies and notes that "we found little evidence to conclude that the purchased services represented increased services or new service programs."[37]

At the same time, services that were given to AFDC recipients dwindled. Part III of the national AFDC study, which deals with services, was not released on time and the delay, according to an HEW official, was due to concern and embarrassment over this fact. The study was conducted in January 1973 and reports that only 43 percent (1,286,650) of AFDC families received one or more services as contrasted with 81 percent (2,041,000) in 1971.[38] The study cautions us not to take this enormous reduction in services seriously as certain reorganizational and redefinitional changes in recording services had taken place. It is clear, however, that there was some decrease in services between the two years, and that the substantial increase in expenditures from 1971 to 1972 must have been for services to nonwelfare recipients.

The states had evidently found what Derthick calls "the worst loophole" in the Social Security Act—the provision for federal grants for social services in a law that called for open-ended funding, loosely-defined services, permission to purchase services from other agencies, and a broad clientele that included former and potential welfare recipients who could be eligible on a "group" basis. But why states took advantage of this law and created a services explosion at this time requires an explanation that takes into account the simultaneous and collusive interests of several relevant groups.

After 1967, the growth of the AFDC rolls continued unabated while the rate of increase in numbers of recipients also accelerated. By 1971 the percent increase over the preceding year was as high as 28.5.[39] The states claimed that they were in financial difficulty and sought additional federal aid, which was found partly in the mechanism of public purchase authorized by the 1962 amendments but not largely used until 1971. The purchase of services from other state agencies by the welfare agency accounted for three-quarters of the rise in expenditures from 1971 to 1972 and increased 17 times during that year. The accounting firm Touche Ross found that "most of these services had been provided as state-funded-and-operated programs prior to their 'purchase' by the public welfare agency."[40]

This was not entire true, however, in the case of child care. In both 1971 and 1972 this was the service with the largest expenditure, rising from $233 million to $409 million within the year.[41] In 1971 child care costs were primarily for welfare agency staff time to arrange such care and for vendor payments to providers of care. While these activities increased in 1972, a large part of the increase in expenditure was also due to child care being purchased from other state agencies. Child care represented the second largest category of public agency purchased services in 1972.[42]

But child care expenditures also expanded because of an increase in private-purchase payments to private agencies for the provision of child care. Private purchase almost doubled between 1971 and 1972 although it explained only 18 percent of the total increase. Nearly half of the private purchase increase was for child care.[43] The 1969 HEW regulation permitting the substitution of private funds for state funds in matching the federal social services grants made it advantageous for private agencies to seek out purchase agreements with welfare agencies. A legislative report in California in 1969 points out how private agencies could make use of the federal law:

> Recent federal legislation offers the potential for improving the planning and funding of private social services. . . . Once the voluntary agency has invested its funds in the central account, the Department of Social and Rehabilitation Service would then contract with that agency to provide its specialized service. A private agency earmarking from its budget the funds . . . can augment that amount with 75% matching funds.[44]

In fact, donated funds did not even need to go through a "central account," in practice. The GAO survey documents how HEW regulations were violated or circumvented. Several contracts with day care centers in Pennsylvania followed this format:

> The State paid these centers an amount comprising the Federal share (75 percent) and the State share, if any. Financial resources of the center, without any transfer of funds from the center to the State, provided the balance.[45]

Private purchase was used for child care as soon as the 1967 amendments and the HEW regulations permitted it, but was greatly expanded between 1971 and 1972, and provided a bonanza for day care centers. Purchased services, both public and private, made up $1.7 billion of the $2.7 billion total services expenditure in 1972. Out of the $409 million for child care, fully $356 million or 87 percent went to purchased services.[46]

The question, of course, arises as to how these interest groups—state legislatures and private agencies that sold services—managed to obtain what they wanted. There had to be a law that permitted expansion, and a federal agency—HEW—to implement it. The HEW services regulations made room for expansion of services into areas outside AFDC and for purposes other than work. But in addition to this, a climate was created by HEW that made this expansion possible. According to Derthick, "the general attitude at the top of CSA [the Community Services Administration of HEW] now and for several years, was that services spending, being of benefit to the poor, should be encouraged to develop as against the day when someone managed to limit it. The stance of CSA was essentially promotional."[47] HEW, indeed, favored the expansion of services and encouraged rather than limited state requests for services funds.

Expansion as a philosophy had its roots not only in the humane tradition that fostered the War on Poverty but in the social work tradition that has as its goal social services for all people. This same professional ideology had been decisive in the establishment of the 1962 services amendments, and although the services methodology in 1967 was no longer casework, the ideal of universal social services still persisted and had its effect on a liberal HEW.

As its 1962 counterpart, the 1967 law appeared to be a tradeoff between a liberal, professionally-oriented HEW and a Congress that was this time even more determined to stop the growth of AFDC through the mechanism of work. And again, services were instituted but meant different things to the two parties. The amendments, for example, made groups of persons who resided in low-income neighborhoods, and other groups, eligible for services. But public assistance and all the benefits accruing from it had always been based on individual (in the adult titles) or family (in AFDC) eligibility. The group eligibility provision ". . . veiled very different purposes. Whereas Congress meant to encourage the welfare poor to go to work, Wilbur Cohen of HEW had taken another step toward the long-range goal of broad provision of social services."[48] The concept of group eligibility was later used by the states to make various groups in institutions eligible for Title IV-A services on the precept that this would prevent individual dependency.

THE 1972 AMENDMENTS: ATTEMPT AT REFORM

The huge growth of social services expenditures in 1972 and the threat of increases in state expenditures for 1973 caused great concern, and in October 1972 Congress passed an amendment that put a $2.5 billion limit on federal social services payments to the states. The new law ruled that 90 percent of these expenditures must be for recipients of cash benefits—public assistance recipients—and only 10 percent could be allocated for services to others. Exempt from this restriction of 90/10 were five categories of services: child care (if used for the purpose of employment of the parent or caretaker or if the mother were dead, absent, or incapacitated and there was no one else to care for the child), services to the mentally retarded and drug addicts, foster care services, and family planning services. The WIN program was altogether excluded from the financial limitation and the 90/10 restriction.

The new law limited social services spending, focused services on recipients of cash payments, and tied more of these services to self-support. But it was ambivalent in that it exempted some services from the 90/10 constraint. The case of child care harbored further mixed motives: child care did not essentially need to be confined to welfare recipients but was limited to purposes of employment and dire necessity. It was left to the secretary of HEW to issue regulations to make the law operable. Casper Weinberger was then secretary of a reorganized HEW oriented to fiscal conservatism and to containing if not reducing the AFDC rolls. HEW was now concerned with correcting the excesses that it had previously allowed. Weinberger interpreted congressional intent in the new law as follows:

> Services available to persons receiving benefits through the AFDC program should be directed toward increasing the employment of heads of AFDC families . . . and, services should be targeted on those persons receiving public assistance or with incomes which placed them in a position that was likely to lead them to dependence on public assistance.[49]

In February of 1973 HEW announced its proposed regulations resulting from the 1972 social services amendment. In line with the Weinberger interpretation, the only goal that the regulations set for social services in AFDC was self-support (the regulations resulting from the 1967 amendment had also listed as a goal "to maintain and strengthen family life"). Mandatory services consisted only of family planning, foster care, and child protection; optional services were day care, educational services, employment services (non-WIN), health-oriented services, homemaker services, home management services, housing improvement services, and transportation. Whereas the former regulations had authorized 21 services, 16 of which were mandatory, these regulations specified 11 services, three of which were mandatory.

The controversial "former and potential" category of persons eligible for services was reduced to those who had been public assistance recipients within the previous three months and those who might become recipients in the next six months. The earlier regulations had specified two and five years respectively. A new criterion for eligibility for services was added: a person's or family's income could not exceed 133⅓ percent of the assistance payment level in the state. No group eligibility was allowed (former regulations contained no income criterion, and group eligibility was permitted).

Child care was made an optional service, except under WIN, where it was continued as mandatory under a different statute. Child care could only be offered "in the absence of another family member who can provide adequate care, and only for the purpose of enabling the caretaker relative (for example, the mother) to accept employment or training or to receive needed services."[50] In the earlier regulations child care was mandatory for working mothers but could be provided for nonworking parents as an optional service. The narrower definition of former and potential clients now also limited child care to families with incomes closer to the AFDC income guidelines. Standards for child care agencies became a matter of meeting state licensing requirements, whereas earlier regulations had stipulated that they also meet the much stricter Federal Interagency Day Care Standards. The practice of purchase of services from public and private agencies was still permitted, but now required written agreements between agencies with prior review by HEW. Donated funds from private sources to substitute for matching state funds were no longer lawful.

The proposed regulations would have reduced the number of required services, restricted eligibility to recipients and near-recipients and eliminated group eligibility, limited child care to children of working mothers and made day care standards less restrictive, and qualified purchase of services and eliminated private matching funds. In essence, the states would have more leeway in determining the number of services they needed to offer, and these services were to be geared to the poor and near-poor and were to be related to employment.

OPPOSITION TO REFORM

These regulations were far from acceptable to the many interest groups that had been benefiting from the earlier regulations. A coalition of 16 national welfare organizations was formed to oppose them, and other groups were mobilized. HEW received over 200,000 letters from over 198,000 individuals and organizations expressing dissension, including congressmen, state governors, state legislators, mayors, university students and faculties, members of labor unions, providers of day care and other services, state and local directors of public welfare, and civic, professional, and religious organizations.

The major complaints against the new regulations concerned goals, eligibility, child care, and donated funds. Social services goals were said to be too narrow, that is, it was felt that the goal of self-support in AFDC should be amplified to include the goal of strengthening family life. Limiting child care to children of working parents only would exclude many children, and the 133⅓ percent of the assistance payment as an eligibility factor was too low. The regulations' definition of "former and potential" recipients was too restrictive. Child care standards should be required to meet the original, more stringent ones, and the prohibition against private donated funds would diminish sources of services, particularly day care for children of working mothers. Doubt was expressed that states could find sufficient tax dollars to make up for the loss of voluntary funds. Interest of the voluntary sector in the needs of the poor would also be diminished.[51]

In the 1972 amendments, Congress had made welfare recipients the primary recipients of social services, but had also exempted such services as child care (if given to working parents) from the restriction to welfare clients. On the other hand, the HEW regulations focused on welfare clients. The Senate Finance Committee, which reviewed these regulations, was concerned that HEW had gone too far in this direction while neglecting the provision that allowed some leeway with such services as child care. Senator Russell Long, chairman of the committee stated that

> portions of the proposed regulations . . . go well beyond last year's legislative action or intent. In particular, the regulations would severely restrict eligibility for child care and family planning which are important services in any effort to help welfare recipients to work their way off welfare and to allow them to remain off welfare.[52]

Despite possible diversion from congressional intent in the regulations, there is some ambiguity as to whether Congress actually changed its mind—its new stand being a result of the heavy pressure exerted by interest groups that were adversely affected by the regulations. Derthick points out that "private agency opposition to the changes was particularly effective. Purchase from private organizations, which was nowhere as important monetarily as purchase from public ones, turned out to be very important politically."[53] If indeed the committee's stance changed in response to public pressure, it was nevertheless couched in terms of prevention of welfare dependency. Senator Walter Mondale, another member of the committee, was concerned that restricting services to welfare recipients and near-recipients—thereby creating a "notch" problem—would act as a disincentive to getting off welfare. If a working recipient were made to pay for child care at a point too close to the welfare payment, he or she might opt to cease work and go on welfare. Similarly, those not on welfare might choose welfare status if only welfare recipients received services.

As a result of these reservations, the committee did not approve the regulations and HEW was directed to revise them by May 1, taking into account the complaints that were received. The revised regulations were also not acceptable, and several subsequent attempts were made by HEW to satisfy Congress, but without success. Finally, the implementation of the 1972 amendments in regard to social services guidelines was postponed by Congress until January 1975.

In the effort to attain congressional approval, HEW liberalized its original regulations several times. The basic revisions in the family services regulations (AFDC—Title IV-A) were in the areas of goals, eligibility, and child care. At the last revision, the goal of "strengthening family life" was added to the self-support goal, which made it possible for child care to be provided "to the extent necessary to accomplish the strengthening family life goal."[54] The controversial child care service was thus extended to families for purposes other than employment, and it had come full circle back to the regulations ensuing from the 1967 amendments, which had allowed care for children of nonworking parents. Day care facilities, in addition to meeting state licensing standards, would also have to meet standards prescribed by the secretary of HEW.

The restriction of eligibility to welfare recipients and near-recipients, another bone of contention, was compromised first by raising the eligibility line for services to 150 percent of the AFDC payment standard, which was higher than the previous 133⅓ percent of the payment level, and finally to 150 percent of the need standard, which was higher still. In addition, $60 per month of earned income could be disregarded in computing eligibility. As for child care, families with above 150 percent and up to 233⅓ percent of the need standard would be partially subsidized. The eligible population was further broadened in the definition of potential AFDC recipients, which was increased from the possibility of welfare status within six months to a period of one year. None of these changes, however, was sufficiently acceptable to permit the regulations to become law.

The struggles around the implementation of the social services law were not accidental, for the issues involved were clear. The major conflicts were: who would be the recipients of services, what the purposes (or goals) of services were, and how widespread services would be.

The question of who was to get services was manifested in the controversy over the designation of a former and potential welfare recipient and in the income level for eligibility. HEW wanted to confine service beneficiaries to welfare and near-welfare levels in order to enable recipients to work their way off welfare (a goal that Congress originally intended), while opponents were interested in extending eligibility to higher income groups. The regulations concerning eligibility were therefore changed accordingly, progressively widening the pool of eligibles by first using the public assistance payment level, then the payment standard, and finally the standard of need. Percent of income above this line was also gradually increased while the definition of former and potential expanded concomitantly. The opponents of the regulations seeking to extend eligibility were, however, interested in the extention of social services to as large a group as possible, since they favored universal services and not services only for the poor or near-poor. These were the professional groups—the voluntary services sector and others who saw social services as a good in itself even without the attendant pragmatic purpose of reducing welfare dependency. They also felt that "services limited to the poor are apt to be inferior."[55]

The conflicting purposes of social services are neatly illustrated in the tension over the regulations' goals. HEW's single goal of self-support and its connection to services such as child care and legal services was intended to reduce welfare dependency. The opposing goal of strengthening family life was, on the contrary, geared toward a therapeutic effort at personal and social rehabilitation. The professional view is expressed by Mayer and Rosenthal, who were concerned that in the regulations "no mention is made of the long-enunciated keystone of social welfare policy in America, the 'strengthening of the family' and the need to keep families intact through supportive, substantive, and supplementary services."[56] This goal, when linked to a service such as child care, results in developmental day care, high standards, and a small select clientele, while child care aimed at constricting the welfare rolls implies custodial day care with less stringent standards and a broader client group.

The issue of how widespread services should be gave rise to disagreement over the number of required and defined services in the regulations, and the dispute over purchase and donations. The opponents of the HEW regulations pressed for both more mandatory services and, failing this, more optional services. The preference was for mandatory services for,

> It is impossible to say how many states will continue these services when there is no compulsion to do so. What is clear is that the federal administration has radically altered its role of leadership in pressing the states for a broader range of services.[57]

In this view, the more services authorized, the more services could be given. Even if federal financing was limited at that moment, services could be increased eventually, as long as the structure existed. Purchase and donations would also enlarge the scope of services. Private purchase and private donations had an additional advantage: they would ensure that the voluntary sector would be the dispenser of services, which would, therefore, be rendered in the best professional manner possible.

State government officials also were in favor of increased federally-authorized services, since federal financial participation relieved the states of the obligation. The strategies of public and private purchase had a similar function. Public purchase meant that federal funds could substitute for state funds in many instances, while private purchase again eased the states' expenditures for services. And, private agency donations, if allowed, could also replace state funds.

THE 1974 AMENDMENTS: RESOLUTION

On January 4, 1975, almost two years after the first HEW regulations were proposed, the Social Services Amendments of 1974 became law, resolving for the moment the long-standing conflict over the future direction of public social services. Title XX of the Social Security Act replaced Title IV-A (and the adult social services title) and was the result of an agreement and coalition between Walter Mondale, Jacob Javits, and other liberal senators, the National Governors' Conference, the representatives of service-rendering social agencies and professional groups, and HEW. HEW, the major proponent of social services for welfare and near-welfare recipients, having come close to the January 1975 deadline without results, finally decided that capitulation and not compromise was in order. The new amendments became effective October 1, 1975.

Title XX can best be understood as a sharp political reaction against the federal regulations of 1973. Three aspects of the 1973 regulations are of interest here: the requirement of tight federal control of state spending; the insistence on a narrow focus of eligibility status (only past, present, or potential welfare recipients were eligible for services); and the interpretation that the primary or perhaps exclusive purpose of a nationwide social service program was that of ending or preventing welfare dependency. The social service community rose up in arms against each of these provisions and the underlying philosophy that informed them. Congress reacted to the pressure and refused to grant permission to HEW to implement the regulations. It was in this context of controversy and contention that the 1974 amendments to the Social Security Act were passed. The *National Journal* described the new law as a "compromise legislation,"[58] but in fact HEW had capitulated on each of the three principles that were embodied in the regulations.

First, the new legislation (Title XX) embodied the principle of state responsibility for social services. The federal government no longer required approval of state plans before they would be funded. The states were to produce annual reports, which the federal government could use to audit to determine if the states had implemented the plans they had projected. National purpose was made subordinate to local initiative on the rationale that the needs of local communities were best interpreted by each state. The "scope of services" clauses of the legislation were hailed as preserving state flexibility while maintaining federal accountability, and indeed the states now had the leeway to decide upon which services they would offer.

Eligibility for services was no longer focused exclusively on welfare status. Three categories were introduced: welfare eligibility, income eligibility, and eligibility without regard to income. However, at least half of the service money had to be spent on the category welfare. This requirement could be met by serving any combination of AFDC, SSI, or Medicaid recipients. The justification for categorical eligibility was that services should be extended both to the working poor and to middle-income families. With this broadening of income eligibility came the principle of fee for services. The rationale was that nonwelfare clients whose income was less than 80 percent of the state median income could qualify for free services, while families with incomes between 80 and 115 percent of the state's median income would be expected to pay all or part of the cost of services. The category of services "without regard to income" was based on the view that all families required some essential services regardless of their income. Universal access was restricted to three services: family planning, protective services, and information and referral services.

The comprehensive program of state-initiated services was intended to attain the following five broad national goals: to help people become or remain economically self-supporting; to help people become or remain self-sufficient; to protect children and adults who cannot protect themselves from abuse, neglect, and exploitation; to help families stay together; to prevent and reduce unnecessary institutional care as much as possible by making home and community services available; and to arrange for appropriate placement and service in an institution when it is in an individual's best interest.

The 1974 legislation resisted earmarking funds for specific programs, instead opting for a strategy of loosely linking services to broad purposes. Under the legislation each service must be directed to at least one of the above goals, and each goal must be furthered by at least one service. However, some recipient groups enjoyed a privileged position; for example, at least three services must be available to SSI beneficiaries. But the pressure for earmarking was strong. In 1978, 1979, and 1980 Congress set aside an additional $200 million specifically for day care, judging this service to be so essential that it made day care available to communities without requiring the local matching of funds.[59]

Private purchase is permitted in the amendments as it was in the HEW regulations, but, unlike in the previous regulations, private donations are also allowed. The private donations clauses read exactly like the regulations stemming from the 1967 amendments, with one exception: federal matching is not available if donated funds revert to the

donor's facility (as before) if the donor is other than a nonprofit orga-
nization. This last stipulation is new and exempts nonprofit agencies
from the restriction against financing their own operations through
federal funds. The voluntary sector could then be directly subsidized by
public funds.

Contracted funds in the voluntary sector may be used to meet the
federal requirement that the states must lay out 25 percent of Title XX
program costs by using both public and private sector expenditures that
are "certified" to be for a Title XX service. Since the goals and categories of eligibility were so broadly defined, most activities can be so
certified.[60] Each of the principles that guided the compromise—the
broadening of eligibility and the differentiation of service goals, the
contracting for services, and the matching funds requirements—oper-
ate to reinforce each other. This situation can be contrasted with the
earlier regulations and legislation, which had created tension between
national and local goals. The "compromise legislation" brought a
measure of harmony to the troubled social service community. However, there was a price to pay for this tranquility: the substantial weakening or, more nearly, the undermining of the goal of services as a work
strategy for AFDC recipients.

A REVIEW OF PAST EXPERIENCE

We turn next to a review of the programmatic experience with services as a work strategy. Ideally, we would like to compare the distribution of work-related services before and after the introduction of Title
XX. But the shift of legislation also brought a different scheme of accounting so that corresponding statistics are not available. Still, the
present data does permit us to construct part of the story. Table 2.1 presents the experience of AFDC clients who did not participate in the
special WIN program, before Title XX legislation was introduced.

In the early years, virtually all AFDC families were reported as having received a service, but this proportion declined sharply from 93
percent in 1969 to 45 percent in 1975. This may not be a decline in actual services but simply a stricter or more realistic assessment of what
activities qualify as a service. Despite these limitations, the figures are
quite interesting. Table 2.1 is limited to those services that might be
broadly interpreted as being related to work, divided into three categories: education, work, and child care. Within the categories, specific
programs are dropped and added. For example, vocational education is
only reported in 1969 and 1971, and literacy training only appears in
1973 and 1975. A review of Table 2.1 shows that the number of recipi-

Table 2.1.
Work-Related Services for all AFDC Families, 1969–75

Type of Service	1969		1971		1973		1975	
	#[a]	%[b]	#	%	#	%	#	%
EDUCATION								
Literacy training	–	–	–	–	19,907	1.5	23,548	1.6
Adult basic education	161,800	10.7	213,800	10.5	137,691	10.7	153,689	6.8
Assistance to children to continue education	452,610	30.0	440,600	21.6	172,500	13.4	108,934	7.2
Vocational education	160,000	10.6	193,900	9.5	–	–	–	–
WORK								
Referral for employment	431,000	28.6	597,800	29.3	335,257	26.1	202,305	13.5
Diagnostic assessment for employment	830,900	55.1	1,030,100	50.5	204,356	15.9	89,502	5.9
Vocational rehabilitation	166,700	11.1	201,300	9.9	100,233	7.8	84,132	5.6
CHILD CARE								
Day care	93,500	6.2	176,400	8.6	281,361	21.9	369,039	24.5
Pre-school education	185,900	12.3	–	–	–	–	–	–
NUMBER OF AFDC FAMILIES RECEIVING A SERVICE	1,508,600		2,041,000		1,286,650		1,503,577	
PERCENT OF ALL AFDC FAMILIES RECEIVING A SERVICE	93		80		43		44	

[a] # of AFDC families receiving this service.
[b] % of all families receiving this service.

Source: U.S. Department of Health, Education and Welfare, SRS, NCSS, *Findings of the 1969 AFDC Study, Part I, "Demographic and Program Characteristics,"* Table 42; U.S. Department of Health, Education and Welfare, SRS, NCSS, *Findings of the 1971 AFDC Study, Part I, "Demographic and Program Characteristics,"* Table 37; U.S. Department of Health, Education and Welfare, SRS, NCSS, *Findings of the 1973 AFDC Study, Part III, "Services to Families,"* Table 4; U.S. Department of Health, Education and Welfare, SSA, ORS, *1975 Recipient Characteristics Study, Part IV, "Social Services,"* Table 3.

ent families for almost all of the education and work services declined in virtually all of the years, while day care services consistently increased. The most striking reductions were in the diagnostic assessment for employment and in referrals for employment. By contrast, the numbers and the proportion of families receiving day care increased sharply from 9 percent in 1969 to 25 percent in 1975.

As the 1967 service amendments were translated into practice, we find less reliance on the so-called soft services of diagnosis and referral. This did not represent a shift to hard services; there was also a decline in the services for basic education and vocational rehabilitation. Even the introduction of the new service category of literacy training did not seem to offset the general pattern. Day care became the major potentially work-related social service for the AFDC family. But since day care serves many purposes, we cannot assume that most day care is a service for working AFDC mothers. All we can infer is that, as the reliance upon education and training services declined steadily, day care increasingly became the central work-related activity.

PRACTICE UNDER TITLE XX

Table 2.2 examines the share of Title XX money and recipients that pertain to AFDC from 1976 through 1980. At the inception of the Title

Table 2.2.
Trends in Title XX by Expenditures and Recipients

	AFDC Recipients	SSI Recipients	Income Eligible*	Universal
	BY EXPENDITURES			
FY 1976	40%	20	32	8
FY 1977	38	22	28	12
FY 1978	31	22	34	13
FY 1979	28	20	37	15
FY 1980	25	20	36	19
	BY RECIPIENTS			
FY 1975	45	19	26	10
FY 1976	31	16	30	23
FY 1978	25	16	29	30
FY 1980	18	11	25	46

*Income Eligible includes Medicaid, which is a minute percentage.

Source: U.S. Department of Health and Human Services, Office of Human Development Services, Office of Social Services Policy, December 4, 1980; internal charts, U.S. Department of Health and Human Services, Office of Human Development Services, Social Services U.S.A. (October–December 1975), p. 2.

XX program, AFDC fared very well but it lost out thereafter in the com-
petition for resources. In 1976, 40 percent of planned expenditures
were set aside for AFDC recipients as compared with only 25 percent in
1980.* The drop is even sharper for the proportion of recipients served
by AFDC. If we accept the first year data available for 1975 as valid,
then we find that there was a decline from 45 percent in 1975 to 18 percent in 1980. Even if the first year statistics are not totally accurate,
comparing 1976 with 1980 we still find a sharp decline from 31 to 18
percent.

As noted earlier, the legislation requires that half of all Title XX
funds be spent on welfare recipients. This stipulation can be met by servicing AFDC, SSI, or Medicaid recipients. We would expect the decline
of expenditures for AFDC to be accompanied by an increase in services
in the SSI and Medicaid categories. However, this did not occur. In the
early years of the program's implementation, over 60 percent of Title
XX funds were expended on welfare recipients. What appears to have
happened is that the universal category "without regard to income"
grew quite sharply from 8 percent to almost one-fifth of total expenditures.

Table 2.3 provides an examination by the three broad work-related
service categories in Title XX of recipients and expenditures as they
comprise proportions of all Title XX recipients and expenditures, and
proportions of all AFDC service recipients and expenditures. These
data are compiled in the official publication entitled *Social Services
U.S.A.*, which is essentially a collation of state services reports to the
Department of Health and Human Services (HHS). There are some gaps
in the data where states have not submitted uniform reports—especially
in the early years—and there is no independent assessment of the activities that are defined as services. Despite these limitations, several interesting patterns do emerge.

First, let us focus on the proportions of work-related services of all
services to those receiving AFDC (columns 2, 4, 6). Three observations
can be made: first, only a small percentage of AFDC service recipients
get education-training and employment services, and over the years the
proportion has declined. Second, a much larger proportion of AFDC
service recipients receive day care, but this has also declined over time
(and as will be discussed below, only a small percentage of the day care

---

*A comparison of actual expenditures shows a drop from 35 percent in 1976 to 29
percent in 1978. There is some evidence to suggest that as the program matured, the
discrepancy between state plans and state outlays declined. If this continued, we can conclude that in the first five years of Title XX implementation, expenditures for AFDC
declined by about 10 percent. (Department of Health and Human Services, Office of
Social Services Policy, personal communication.)

Table 2.3.
Trends in Work-Related Services under Title XX by Primary Recipients and Expenditures

PRIMARY RECIPIENTS

Work-Related Service Categories	1975 First Quarter		1977 Third Quarter		1978 Third Quarter	
	(1) AFDC %[a]	(2) % of AFDC[b]	(3) AFDC %	(4) % AFDC	(5) AFDC %	(6) % AFDC
Day care	62.6	23.4	46.3	19.9	47.4	20.8
Education and training	46.0	8.4	36.8	6.6	31.1	5.8
Employment	60.8	8.2	39.2	5.3	38.9	4.3
Total (all AFDC service recipients)	1,098		1,188		1,103	

EXPENDITURES

Work-Related Service Categories	1976 Third Quarter		1977 Third Quarter		1978 Third Quarter	
Day care	46.0	33.0	48.0	36.0	44.6	37.4
Education and training	27.0	5.0	21.0	4.7	13.0	3.4
Employment	43.0	5.0	16.0	1.8	22.0	2.6

[a]Percentage of total Title XX service categories.
[b]Percentage of AFDC total.

Source: U.S. Department of Health and Human Services, Office of Human Development Services, Office of Social Services Policy, Social Services U.S.A., Statistical Tables, Summaries and Analyses of Services Under Social Security Act Titles XX, IV-B, and IV-A/C for Fifty States and D.C. (October–December 1975, July–September 1976, 1977, 1978).

service is actually work-related). Third, when we turn to expenditures, much the same pattern can be seen in education-training and employment services. Despite the declining proportion of AFDC service recipients using day care, however, this service has absorbed a rising percentage of funds.

When we look at where AFDC work-related services fit into the overall Title XX program, (columns 1,3,5) we find a similar pattern to the one above. With the passage of time, AFDC service recipients and expenditures accounted for a smaller proportion of Title XX recipients and funds expended. This is true for all three work-related service categories: day care, education-training, and employment. The declines are sharper in program participation than in financial outlays, the most dramatic change being in expenditures for employment services. It is striking to note that a corollary expansion of funds for employment services for non-AFDC service recipients of from 57 percent to 78 percent took place between 1976 and 1978.

It is obvious from these figures that by 1978, the AFDC claim on the work-related services in Title XX was substantially weakened, although the expenditures for day care decreased only modestly. While the rates of decline varied programwide for both service recipients and funds, AFDC accounted for less than half of total Title XX resources in each program category.

Day care was a central category both before and after Title XX, and it plays a critical role in relation to work for AFDC mothers. As can be seen in Table 2.3, in all years less than half of Title XX day care expenditures went for AFDC recipients while the remainder was non-AFDC related. The question now as before is to what extent are such day care services provided to working mothers?

The publication *Social Services U.S.A.* sheds some light on this matter. In the reporting quarters between October 1976 and September 1977, the quarterly averages were as follows: of all day care costs, 47 percent went for AFDC recipients, which included 32 percent for "AFDC Training and Job-related" and 15 percent for "other AFDC." Income eligibles captured as much as 44 percent of day care expenditures. In effect only a third of day care funds were related to work. As for the proportions of children receiving the day care service, 38 percent were "AFDC Training and Job-related" while 21 percent were AFDC recipients but not the children of working or training mothers, and 40 percent were "income eligible." Less than 40 percent of such children were in day care for reasons of employment.[61]

A more personal study provides an even less optimistic estimate. HEW considered shifting from direct funding of day care providers through Title XX to allowing exemptions for clients who purchased their own day care services. In the study, AFDC day care recipients were sampled in two states and it was discovered that despite reports that 85 percent of these mothers were receiving such services for work-related reasons, in fact only a quarter of them were actually wage earners.[62] These figures, if applied nationally, suggest that even among AFDC families where day care is reported as given for purposes of employment, it is instead being dispensed for other reasons.

Why again, as after 1967, does such a small proportion of the day care service find its way to the working mother on AFDC, who is ostensibly one of the prime intended recipients of Title XX funds. Most informed opinion believes that the legislation that permitted subcontracting day care to private providers is an important factor. The assumption is that providers do not want to serve AFDC clients, and when provider preferences are influential, practice follows accordingly. This phenomenon has not been curbed because of the inability of states to impose their preferences on the private provider.[63] The result has been a provider-dominated market affording services that are not relevant to the working AFDC mother.

Some factual information pertinent to this argument indicates that in 1977 a little less than half of Title XX expenditures for day care services went to private contractors.[64] Concern about this state of affairs has led some states, notably Massachusetts, to consider the feasibility of increasing the work-related income exemption for the AFDC wage earner and eliminating or reducing the funding of day care from Title XX funds. Such a change in policy, according to the REAP report, an HEW sponsored study, would enable states to "free far more Title XX dollars for reallocation than they would spend on increased AFDC payments."[65] The intended consequence, of course, is the provision of more day care services to AFDC mothers in order to enable them to work.

CONCLUSIONS

The new amendments (Title XX) contained goals beyond self-support for AFDC recipients: they extended eligibility to the middle-income population, created a structure for many kinds of services, and made possible the public support of private agencies. These changes clearly indicated the future course of social services. As we have seen, social services under Title XX were even less geared to enable employment for the AFDC mother than social services under Title IV-A (AFDC). By 1980 service recipients in the universal category "without regard to income" became the largest group receiving Title XX funds.

Since 1962, the avowed purpose of social services in public assis-

tance has been to reduce public dependency. While in 1962 rehabilitation was to lead to this goal, in 1967 the mechanism for achieving it
overtly became work. In 1974, the same rationale appeared in a statement Senator Lloyd Bentsen made in introducing the Senate version of
the amendments: ". . . the purpose of the social service program is to
reduce welfare dependency by providing Federal assistance to a wide
range of services intended to move recipients into self-sufficiency."[66]
Senator Mondale added, "by providing child care to children of working parents, the program can reduce the welfare rolls."[67] We have seen,
however, that the child care service did not go to many working parents
within AFDC, and that among the "former and potential" recipients a
substantial part of it served nonworking parents, even under the old
law.

Title XX created a situation even further removed from the goal of
reducing dependency. While it still limited federal participation to $2.5
billion nationally, it brought a whole new higher-income population into the social services recipient network. The income discrepancy between the new recipients and the recipients of AFDC is enormous.
Since 50 percent of expenditures must, by law, go for services to
welfare recipients, the remaining 50 percent is left for nonrecipients
with annual incomes that start right above the welfare breakeven point
and climb to as high as $16,000. It was reasonable to expect that in the
period from 1975 to 1980, among potential services recipients, those
with the highest incomes would co-opt the major part of social services.

The situation emerged from a coalition of providers and users of
services. The higher-income groups with more political power did not
find it difficult to obtain scarce social service funds. And the voluntary
sector, now the main provider of services, which has traditionally not
served the very poor, "creamed" the higher-income groups to obtain
clients more receptive to its therapeutic methods and rehabilitative
goals. As a result, social services as a strategy to promote work among
AFDC recipients never became a reality. The question of whether such
a strategy would have been effective cannot be answered, given the experience of the last fifteen years.

NOTES

1. Charles E. Gilbert, "Policy-Making in Public Welfare," *Political Science Quarterly*
81 (June 1966), p. 209.

2. Irene Lurie, "An Economic Evaluation of Aid to Families with Dependent Children," mimeographed (Washington, D.C.: The Brookings Institution, 1968), p. 46.

3. U.S. Department of Health, Education and Welfare, *Public Assistance 1962* (Washington, D.C.; 1962), p. 2.

4. Lurie, "An Economic Evaluation," p. 45.

5. Gilbert, "Policy-Making," p. 199.

6. U.S. Department of Health, Education and Welfare, *Report on the Implementation and Results of the 1962 Service Amendments to the Public Assistance Titles*, (Washington, D.C., 1964), p. 4.

7. Ibid.

8. Ibid., p. 9.

9. U.S. Department of Health, Education and Welfare, Social and Rehabilitation Service, National Center for Social Statistics, *Findings of the 1967 AFDC Study*, Table 71.

10. U.S. Department of Health, Education and Welfare, Social and Rehabilitation Service, National Center for Social Statistics, *Characteristics of Families Receiving Aid to Families with Dependent Children, November–December 1961*, Table 12.

11. *Findings of the 1967 AFDC Study*, Table 23.

12. U.S. Department of Health, Education and Welfare, Social and Rehabilitation Service, National Center for Social Statistics, *Trend Report: Graphic Presentation of Public Assistance and Related Data*, 1969, p. 27.

13. U.S. Congress, Senate, Committee on Finance, *Hearings on Regulations of the Department of Health, Education and Welfare Concerning Social Services Funded Under the Social Security Act*. 93d Cong., 1st sess., 1973, pp. 58–69.

14. U.S. Department of Health, Education and Welfare, Social and Rehabilitation Service, National Center for Social Statistics, *Findings of the 1971 AFDC Study*, Table 37.

15. Joel F. Handler, and Jane Ellen Hollingsworth, *The "Deserving Poor" A Study of Welfare Administration* (Chicago: Markham, 1971), p. 107.

16. Ibid., pp. 127, 126.

17. *Findings of the 1971 AFDC Study*, Table 37.

18. *Hearings on Regulations Concerning Social Services*, p. 128.

19. *Findings of the 1971 AFDC Study*, Table 83.

20. Ibid.

21. Ibid.

22. U.S. Department of Health, Education and Welfare, Social and Rehabilitation Service, National Center for Social Statistics, *Findings of the 1973 AFDC Study*, Part III, Table 14.

23. Ibid., Part I, Tables 33 and 51.

24. Ibid., Part III, Table 3.

25. U.S. Department of Labor, Manpower Administration, *Evaluation of Supportive Services Provided for Participants of Manpower Programs*, prepared by Camil Associates, Philadelphia, 1972, p. 53.

26. Office of Economic Opportunity, *Day Care Survey 1970*, prepared by the Westinghouse Learning Corporation, Westat Research Incorporated, (Washington, D.C.: WLC-Westat Research, Inc., 1971).

27. Charles L. Schultze, Edward R. Fried, Alice M. Rivlin, Nancy H. Teeters, *Setting National Priorities, the 1973 Budget* (Washington, D.C.: The Brookings Institution, 1972), pp. 262, 263.

28. Irene Lurie, "Legislative, Administrative and Judicial Changes in the AFDC Program, 1967–71," *Studies in Public Welfare*, Paper no. 5, Part 2, *Issues in Welfare Administration-Intergovernmental Relationships*, prepared for the Joint Economic Committee, U.S. Congress, Washington, D.C.: 1973, p. 74.

29. *Some Problems in Contracting for Federally-Assisted Child Care Services*, General Accounting Office, Report to the Congress, June 1973, p. 23.

30. Blanche Bernstein, "Day Care," *Studies in Public Welfare*, Paper no. 8; *Income-Tested Social Benefits in New York: Adequacy, Incentives, and Equity*, prepared for the Joint Economic Committee, U.S. Congress, Washington, D.C., 1973, p. 113.

31. Ibid., p. 111.

32. *Some Problems in Contracting for Child Care Services*, p. 16.

33. Ibid., pp. 1,2.

34. Ibid., p. 16.

35. Martha Derthick, *Uncontrollable Spending for Social Services* (Washington, D.C.: Brookings Institution, 1975), p. 8.

36. *Hearings on Regulations Concerning Social Services*, p. 128.

37. Ibid., p. 119.

38. *Findings of the 1973 AFDC Study*, Part III, Table 3.

39. U.S. Department of Health, Education and Welfare, Social and Rehabilitation Service, National Center for Social Statistics, *AFDC: Selected Statistical Data on Families Aided and Program Operations*, June 1971, Item 26, Table 1.

40. *Hearings on Regulations Concerning Social Services*, pp. 118, 119.

41. Ibid., p. 128.

42. Ibid., p. 120.

43. Ibid., p. 122.

44. Derthick, *Uncontrollable Spending*, p. 33.

45. *Some Problems in Contracting for Child Care Services*, p. 32.

46. *Hearings on Regulations Concerning Social Services*, pp. 130, 131.

47. Derthick, *Uncontrollable Spending*, p. 38.

48. Ibid., p. 15.

49. *Hearings on Regulations Concerning Social Services*, p. 9.

50. Ibid., p. 63.

51. *Federal Register* 38, no. 83 (May 1, 1973), p. 10782.

52. *Hearings on Regulations Concerning Social Services*, p. 2.

53. Derthick, *Uncontrollable Spending*, p. 103.

54. *Federal Register*, p. 30074.

55. Anna Mayer and Marguerite Rosenthal, "The Poor Get Poorer: Making the Family Impossible," in *What Nixon is Doing to Us*, eds. Alan Gartner, Colin Greer, and Frank Reissman (New York: Harper and Row, 1973), p. 23.

56. Ibid., p. 19.

57. Ibid., p. 21.

58. Joel Havemann, "Welfare Report Impasse over Social Services Regulations Appears Broken," *National Journal Reports* (December 7, 1974), p. 1840.

59. U.S. Department of Health and Human Services, Office of Human Development Services *Annual Report to the Congress on Title XX of the Social Security Act Fiscal Year 1979* (Washington, D.C.: Office of the Secretary, 1980), p. viii.

60. Ibid., pp. 1840 to 1844 (all Title XX legislation is indicated in this source).

61. U.S. Department of Health, Education and Welfare, Office of Human Development Services, *Social Services, U.S.A.*, Annual Summary, October 1976 to September, 1977, pp. 30, 33.

62. *Policy Implications of Alternative Child Care Funding Mechanisms*, Executive Summary (Washington, D.C.: REAP Associates, June 1977), p. 2.

63. See Barbara Wishnov, *Can State Government Gain Control?* (Boston: Massachusetts Taxpayers Foundation, January 1980).

64. *Social Services U.S.A.*, p. 60.

65. *Policy Implications of Alternative Child Care Funding Mechanisms*, p. 2.

66. U.S. Congress, Senate, *Congressional Record*, 93rd Congress, 2nd Session, October 3, 1974, p. S18166.

67. Ibid., p. S18164.

3

Work Through Incentives

Concurrent with the effort to promote work through social services was the emphasis starting in the 1960s on work incentives. An incentive strategy is based on the assumption that if recipients are permitted to keep part of their earnings they will find it worthwhile to work; heads of AFDC families would then act "rationally" and choose to work if it were to their economic advantage.

Work incentives had been in effect prior to 1960 in the AFDC programs of the southern states but were not clearly enunciated as a national policy for the allowance of exempted work expenses until 1962. In 1967, a formal across-the-board thirty and one-third disregard of earnings was legislated as a further attempt to induce work through incentives. During the late 1960s and the 1970s, incentives were a critical aspect of welfare reform proposals such as the Family Assistance Plan (FAP) and President Carter's Better Jobs and Incomes Program (BJIP) and also formed the basis of the negative income tax (NIT) experiments where varying combinations of "tax rates" (incentives) and benefit levels (guarantees) were employed to ascertain their effect on work effort.

This chapter will review both the programmatic experience with work incentives in AFDC and the results of the NIT experiments. These two programs are not quite parallel for two reasons. First, very little research has been conducted to arrive at the effects of work incentives on AFDC recipients while the NIT experiments yielded an enormous amount of interest and data analysis. Second, the concerns of each set of incentives were also quite different. In the AFDC program the goal was to encourage AFDC recipients to start to work or, if already working, to work more. The NIT experiments were undertaken to see

47

whether providing incentive payments would reduce work activity among those already in the labor force. Nevertheless, both purposes have a bearing on incentives. Since it is work for the heads of AFDC families that was the concern of policy makers, we will focus on this aspect of the work incentives strategy.

BUDGETING INCENTIVES

Incentives in the form of earnings exemptions were present in the southern states and in some western states well before this became a national policy. In these states, only a proportion of the family's need was granted by the welfare agency, and all or part of the earnings between what the agency paid and what was defined as need were disregarded. The recipient was therefore strongly motivated to work since a substantial amount of additional income could be earned without a reduction in the welfare grant. There was, however, another incentive that encouraged work—the low level of welfare benefits in many of these states. AFDC mothers were almost compelled to work by the sheer necessity for additional income. Together, high disregards and low assistance grants acted as powerful motivators to work. While this situation existed only in certain states, Hausman estimated that "a substantial minority" of recipients lived in such states,[1] while Carter wrote that there were twenty such states representing 25 percent of the national AFDC caseload.[2]

WORK EXPENSES

The 1962 amendments to the AFDC title of the Social Security Act legislated the exclusion of work expenses in the computation of a family's welfare budget. Some states had been disregarding work expenses before 1962; the amendment made it mandatory for all states to do so, but left it to the states to define work expenses. As a result, in the early years, allowances for work expenses varied tremendously from state to state. Some states included child care and work-related taxes such as social security while others did not. Some states had flat allowances for work expenses while others treated this item on an "as incurred" basis. Other states had a work allowance that was an automatic stipend for employed recipients, for example, $20 per month in Michigan. New York City's variant of this was the "basic food allowance," which was higher for employed recipients than for others.

A 1968 survey of ten states indicated a wide range of such allowable exemptions: from no work expenses other than child care in North Carolina to all work expenses including union dues, uniforms, transportation, etc., as incurred, in New York.[3] Lurie's 1973 study of work expenses in seven states revealed that work expenses allowed increased on a continuum of from 18 to 47 cents with each dollar earned among the seven states. In addition to statutory differences, as Heffernan points out, "another major source of unintended variance is the degree of caseworker discretion currently practiced in the administration of public assistance . . . some pro-client caseworkers take pride in generating enough expenses so that allowable income falls to zero. . . ."[5]

In many states, work expenses add up to a substantial amount of money. In Wisconsin, an automatic $40 per month is exempted for work expenses, and additional expenses can be deducted as needed. Handler and Hollingsworth describe a "typical expense allowance" for a month in one county as the automatic $40 work expense, $64 for child care, $10 for transportation, and $2 for miscellaneous items, or $116 in all.[6] Nationally, the average monthly amount of disregarded employment expenses, excluding child care, is $82.95.[7] Aside from the fact that working recipients are reimbursed for expenses incurred as a result of working, they receive an additional bonus to the extent to which allowable work expenses exceed the actual costs of being employed. Work expenses, therefore, have a dual incentive function in many instances.

THIRTY AND ONE-THIRD

National policy to encourage work through incentives began in 1962 but the 1967 amendments to the Social Security Act greatly extended this policy. In 1967 it became mandatory that each state disregard a certain portion of recipients' earnings, for the explicit purpose of inducing work. Economists had been under the impression that work in public assistance had heretofore carried a 100 percent benefit-loss rate (to which they now applied the term tax rate); that is, for every dollar earned an equivalent dollar was deducted from the assistance payment. It seemed obvious that such rules would inhibit work effort and they proposed measures to institute work incentives in the form of earnings exemptions. They recommended, in short, that the tax rate on earnings be reduced. (Their assumption in fact was erroneous. As noted earlier, several states had disregarded income from work through their method of budgeting.) The 1967 disregard of earned income, effective in July 1969, was the first major piece of legislation reflecting this theory of economic rationalism.

The law stipulates that the first $30 per month of earnings plus one-third of the remainder will be exempted as income to be counted toward reducing the assistance payment. This only affects families already on AFDC. A family that is applying for welfare must be eligible without the disregard; its income must fall below the grant level, not considering the disregard. The rule disregarding earned income cannot be a test of eligibility outside the system but it does afford a bonus to those within it. This distinction is important, for the purpose of the amendment is to encourage those on welfare to work, not to encourage those at work to become welfare-eligible.

CASUAL INCOME

There is still another type of disregard that may act as a work incentive. This concerns income earned on an irregular or sporadic basis, which cannot be depended upon for continued and total support of the family but nevertheless increases total income. Piore says of this supplementary income that, although it "may enable some families to live well above the welfare standard, the welfare payment is probably essential to the families' survival."[8]

This kind of nonrecurring income can be disregarded in three different ways. It may not be budgeted, not reported by the caseworker, or not reported by the client. Some states take the first option: they legitimate a route by which such income can be declared but not budgeted. In Massachusetts this is "casual income" and is defined as any amount that is "not received periodically or continuously" and that "cannot be computed or predicted over a period of time." In Wisconsin it is called "inconsequential income." This kind of disregard may encourage the client to choose sporadic and irregular work rather than regular work.

When supplementary income is not legitimated, it still may be disregarded by the caseworker. Handler and Hollingsworth found that in Wisconsin many working mothers "kept a good deal of their earnings," that the earned-income policy was not being uniformly enforced, and that caseworkers tended to exercise their discretion and treat a great deal of earned income as "inconsequential," whether or not it technically fell into that category. Handler and Hollingsworth further speculated that "because of lack of enforcement, the earned-income policy [deducting the equivalent of earned income from the welfare payment] does not have a disincentive effect."[9]

The third route for disregarding supplementary or irregular income is the failure of the client to report it. The kind of work performed to earn irregular or sporadic income is equally irregular or sporadic and lends itself to a flexibility of disclosure that is consistent with not reporting. In addition, the welfare machinery for budgeting such income—a system geared to regular budget deduction—would leave the recipient's grant continuously confused and in a state of arrears if such income were conscientiously reported. This is probably why some states have instituted a legitimate route for not budgeting such income.

The treatment of recurring earned income as casual income may contribute to wide variations in tax rates among states. In 1967, economists Barr and Hall did an empirical study of actual tax rates in nine major cities and found that on $100 of monthly earnings, the rates at which AFDC recipients were taxed ranged from 18 percent to 72 percent. It was also apparent that these rates were lower than statutory requirements called for. Barr and Hall surmised that tax rates may be even lower than their figures indicate since the "results measure the implicit tax rates that caseworkers think they are imposing and may exceed the tax rates as perceived by family members to the extent that they are able to conceal their true earnings from the caseworker." They conclude that there are "relatively low tax rates on earned income under AFDC" and that "the prevailing belief that the system of public assistance imposes a nearly confiscatory tax on earnings needs substantial revision."[10] Lurie, too, notes that "the estimated rates on earnings are low, rarely higher than 50 percent," and that they vary tremendously.[11]

Williams, who analyzed the data from the ten-state study mentioned earlier, found that "The tax rates . . . are considerably lower than we would expect from the formal structures of the AFDC programs in the ten states. . . . The coefficients on earnings imply average tax rates ranging from a low of 11 percent in Georgia to a high of 57 percent in New York."[12] These findings are particularly interesting because five of the ten states studied ostensibly had a 100 percent legal tax rate on earnings while the other five had a lower earnings reduction rate. In both cases, however, actual exemptions far exceeded the formal requirements. Williams attributes this anomaly to caseworker proclivity to overlook certain earnings.

It is clear from our review of programmatic practices that taken together, budgeting disregards, work expense deductions, the formal thirty and one-third exemption, and informal disregards of casual and recurring earnings add up to a substantial amount of additional income that can be accumulated by the AFDC recipient as a result of working. What is not equally clear is to what extent these practices influenced the work behavior of AFDC family heads—mostly mothers. Do these exemptions of earned income in fact act as work incentives, encouraging those who do not work to enter the labor market and those at work to work more? The next section will review what is known about this question by referring both to the national data and the limited number of empirical studies. Since the major national policy innovation in the work incentive strategy was the thirty and one-third earnings exemption, we will examine the impact of this policy on work effort both before and after 1969, the date that the 1967 legislation became effective.

WORK EXPERIENCE BEFORE 1969

In spite of differences among states in exemptions for work expenses, in the treatment of casual income, and in the degree of caseworker discretion, the major cause of variations in tax rates is due to diversity in budgeting earned income. Even before work became an issue in welfare policy, some observers discovered that in states that practiced method-of-budgeting disregards, more recipients worked. As early as 1960, Schorr noted that in 1958, of 34 states with a maximum payment or other such limitation on benefits, 23 states had an average of more than 10 percent of their mothers working and 11 states had a work average that was less than this. Conversely, of 16 states without a maximum, only two states had more than 10 percent working while 14 states had less. He infers that "states that provide this small measure of incentives show an increased percentage of working mothers over those that do not."[13] The incentive in the first group of states was the practice that earnings between the maximum payment and what the state considered the "need standard" were either fully or partially disregarded; tax rates in these states were therefore lower than in the second group of states.

Carter, examining the 1961 AFDC survey, pointed to the fact that while the national average of working mothers was 14 percent, in states with an earnings exemption the median was 22 percent while in those states without an exemption the median was only 6 percent. She explains this dramatic difference as follows:

> on the one hand, women on AFDC are highly motivated to work when grants are low and earnings exemptions are allowed . . . demonstrating the value of employment incentives. On the other hand, States that attempt to meet 100 percent of State standards . . . do not have the same high rate of employment. . . . Obviously, employment incentives such as earnings exemptions for *life survival* have a different meaning from employment incentives for *upward mobility*.[14] (Emphasis in original)

Cox, reporting on the situation in 1967, showed that the median proportion of working mothers in states with earnings exemptions was 28.3

percent, compared with a median of 10.5 percent in the other states. She adds, like Carter, that those states with work incentives were "States with relatively low AFDC payments; consequently, economic pressure to acquire additional income was considerable."[15]

Schorr, Carter, and Cox recognized that both incentives and low assistance payments played a part in producing differential work effort among states, but their research did not attempt to evaluate the relative weight of each determinant. Furthermore, it is conceivable that other factors, such as the administrative emphasis on work as a policy and agricultural economics where there is a demand for low-wage, un-skilled labor, resulted in increased work effort in the low-benefit, high-incentive states.

More recently, Garfinkel and Orr, using cross-sectional aggregate state data for 1967, attempted to discern the effect of both tax rates and guarantees (benefit levels) on the employment of AFDC mothers. Their regression analysis yielded the following results: a 10 percent reduction in the tax rate (a 10 percent increase in total earned income disre-garded) would lead to a 7 percent increase in the employment rate of AFDC mothers. And a 10 percent increase in the guarantee would in-duce a 7 percent decrease in the employment rate. While these figures look promising, we are cautioned that "the percentage changes in the employment rate appear large while the absolute changes appear small because the mean employment rate—18 percent—is so low."[16] It ap-pears that tax rates and benefit levels had a similar effect on work ef-fort, which varied negatively with both by the same amount.

WORK EXPERIENCE AFTER 1969

The thirty and one-third earnings exemption was the first signifi-cant federal effort to mandate work incentives. Analysts have shown little interest in the systematic evaluation of programmatic practice, favoring instead the assessment of the negative income tax social ex-periments. We have provided an overview of the effects of the earnings exemption on work behavior, making use of data in the national AFDC surveys and in empirical studies.

The first question to ask of the national data is whether more cases are closed for employment of the mother now that thirty and one-third has been in effect for some time. If the disregard was successful, we might expect that as more AFDC mothers start to work or work more, more of their cases will be discontinued. In actuality, however, it turns out that the findings are reversed. In July to December 1965, 1966, 1967, and 1968 cases closed for employment or increased earnings of the mother ranged from 12.3 to 13.5 percent of all closings.[17] In 1969, the first year of the disregard, only 7.7 percent of closings were for this reason and approximately this proportion exemplified all of the subsequent years, through 1979, so that, the thirty and one-third earnings exemption appears to have almost halved the percentage of closings for employment.[18]

This can be explained by the fact that due to the now higher "breakeven point" the earnings exemption permitted workers with more earnings to remain on AFDC who would not have been eligible for continued assistance before. Thus, fewer of these cases were closed. This would lead us to believe then that there should be more employed mothers in the caseload after the disregard than there were before. But the evidence does not support this thesis. The percent of all AFDC families that have female heads who are employed has remained almost constant from 1961 through 1977; during the 1960s about 13 percent of mothers worked,[19] in 1971 there were 13.9 percent.[20] In 1973 this figure rose somewhat to 16 percent[21] but by 1977 the proportion declined again to 13.8 percent[22] or about the same rate as prevailed in 1971. The disregard then appeared to have had little effect on proportions of employed AFDC family heads.

The proportion of mothers in the "employed" status remained basically the same, while "case closings for employment" declined sharply. Both of these findings are related to each other. A mother is counted as employed for one of two reasons: either she is working and not earning enough, so AFDC supplements her earnings, or she has started to work recently and is only awaiting a salary check or some administrative action before her case will be closed. If more mothers were at work after the disregards than before, this should be reflected both in the proportion continuously at work and in the proportion in the process of being terminated from AFDC. The terminating group should show up first in the employed figure and then in the "case closings" figure. Even if fewer cases proportionately are being closed as a result of the higher breakeven point—the point at which income exceeds need and the case is closed—due to the disregard, then more of these cases should be reflected in the account of those employed. Since the latter is not the case, it would appear that not only are there no more women at work, but in fact there may be fewer, since the lower case closing rate does not result in a higher employed rate.

The national data do not lend support to the thesis that the thirty and one-third disregard had a positive effect on work effort. This is even more surprising in light of the fact that AFDC mothers have become more employable through the years. Both educational and skill levels have risen. In 1967, for example, 18.0 percent of these women had completed high school or attended college. A decade later, in 1977, the proportion increased to 24.0 percent. When we compare the trends in the occupational position of AFDC mothers, we find that the proportion of white collar, skilled blue collar, and service industry workers increased between 1967 and 1977. By contrast, in the same period, the proportion of laborers and private household workers declined sharply. Family size, another important dimension of employability, has also decreased: from 1967 to 1977 the median number of children per AFDC family declined from 3.2 to 2.2.[23]

Although female head recipients have become personally more employable, the rising tide of general unemployment might tend to undercut this factor. The unemployment rate among women who head families rose from 4.9 percent in 1967, climbing steadily until it reached 10 percent in 1975 and 1976, and then declined to 9.3 in 1977.[24] Although there has been some question about the extent of the relationship between the work activity of AFDC mothers and overall unemployment rates, Erie, Fisher, and Dayan note that in times of very high unemployment, as in the 1970s, "the program's increased responsiveness to aggregate joblessness became apparent . . . changes in unemployment were felt more quickly by the welfare system."[25]

In summary, we must say that in spite of the increased employability of AFDC mothers, the national data show that work effort, as measured by those at work while on welfare and cases closed for employment, did not increase after the institution of the thirty and one-third earnings exemption. The national data consider all states and yield average results. It is important therefore to examine local studies as well since these may show differing effects of the disregard in different areas. There have, however, been few empirical studies to test the results of the earnings exemption.

The National Analysts, Inc. did a cross-country survey at the request of HEW and published their results in May 1972. Two waves of interviews were conducted; the first in 1969, when the disregard had been in effect for six months, of 3,508 AFDC mothers in ten cities; the second wave in 1971 of 2,425 of the same women. Cities with different labor market conditions were chosen to test the effect of this variable. At the end of the first interview each respondent was given a detailed explanation of the disregard policy so that ostensibly all of them were knowledgeable about it in the period between the first and the second interview.

Since it is essential for AFDC mothers to know about a work incentive in order for it to be effective, knowledge of the disregard was one of the two principal effects that the survey tested. During the first set of interviews almost half of the women were not aware of the earnings exemption and expressed the belief that if they obtained a job that paid as much as the welfare check, they would lose the check entirely. During the second series of interviews, fully one-third of the respondents were still under this misapprehension, although they had all been informed otherwise by the interviewer.[26]

The fate of work effort fared as badly. During both waves of interviews the same proportion of women, two-fifths, were either working, looking for work, or enrolled in training programs. Only one-quarter of them were actually working at the time of both interviews. As was expected, employment rates were higher in good labor market sites than in poor ones. When work motivation was considered, as described by the respondents themselves, the picture was even bleaker. Only 13 percent said they had looked for work because of the earnings exemption, and less than half of these said they had started to work because of it. None of them had left welfare as a result of the new policy and fully four-fifths of the women said they had engaged in no work-related behavior as a consequence of the disregard.

The study concludes that ". . . for women, at least, the Earnings Exemption has been ineffective in compelling recipients into the labor force or into job training," and "the Earnings Exemption failed to act as a work incentive for the population it was designed to motivate."[27] It goes on to speculate that the lack of a financial incentive is not the only major barrier to employment in the AFDC population and that in fact it may never have been a barrier for many recipients.

Not all studies come to so grim a conclusion. The Appel and Schlenker analysis of work effort in 13 Michigan counties used secondary data and studied the period between July 1969 and July 1970 in an attempt to test the effect of the disregard. They found that female employment did increase during this period from 7 percent to 12.1 percent of all AFDC families. In addition, a longitudinal sample of 3,831 women who were on AFDC in both July 1969 and July 1970 was also examined and yielded a 70 percent net increase in employed women at the later point in time.[28]

While the National Analysts study was concerned mainly with awareness of the disregard policy, the Appel and Schlenker exploration was heedful of additional factors. The problem was to isolate the effect of the earnings exemption in order to determine whether it caused the increase in employment. There are several potential barriers to this process. Such structural dimensions as ignorance of the disregard, lack of jobs, transportation, and child care facilities, and poor health would all qualify employment rates. It is even more difficult to isolate the effect of the disregard statistically since the exemption causes the breakeven point to rise, thereby keeping more employed recipients in the caseload and increasing the proportion of those employed. What needs to be measured, then, is new employment, to ascertain whether work behavior has increased.

The researchers attempted to differentiate new employment by taking the July 1970 figure of those employed and deducting from that figure those women who would have been off assistance had their earnings been above the level permitted in July 1969. The adjustment reduced the increase in employment in all geographic areas, but in nine of the 13 areas the increase over July 1969 was still statistically significant. This device brought the issue of earnings into focus. Earnings increased between 1969 and 1970 from $176 to $191 per month. Average earnings increased in 10 of the 13 areas, "but it is unclear whether this is a significant increase caused by the work incentive."[29] As in the national data, case closings for employment fell from 33 percent to 23 percent in the one year, indicating that those with higher earnings were retained in the caseload. Increases in earnings are like increases in employment: it is difficult to separate out higher earnings from the fact that higher earnings were now permissible as a result of the higher breakeven point created by the disregard.

Unfortunately, Appel and Schlenker failed to test their results in the context of trend data. Their conclusion that employment rose between 1969 and 1970 because of the disregard is mitigated by examining employment in Michigan prior to 1969. The national AFDC surveys present a picture of 10.8 percent AFDC mothers employed in Michigan in 1961, 12.4 percent in 1967, 5.6 percent in 1969, and 9.4 percent in 1971.[30] Apparently in May 1969, when the national survey was taken, AFDC employment in the state was at an all-time low. The fact that it rose after this and did not even reach the proportion in 1971 (9.4 percent) that it had in 1961 and 1967 seems to give no special credit to the disregard policy. It is difficult too to attribute any increase in earnings to the disregard, since the average monthly earnings of AFDC mothers in Michigan continued to rise from $59.32 in 1961 to $129.38 in 1967 and $196.68 in 1971.[31]

In spite of uncertainties in the evidence presented and the difficulties in isolating the effects of the disregard on work effort both pragmatically and statistically, Appel and Schlenker nevertheless conclude that the earnings exemption had a positive outcome in the 13 counties they reviewed in Michigan. Given all these qualifications, the observer is hard pressed to agree with their conclusion. The results of their analysis can be criticized even more concretely on the grounds that they did not allocate their findings to a historical context. It is therefore questionable whether the disregard policy had a positive effect on work activity in Michigan.

A more recent analysis by Friedman and Hausman of national data from the Panel Study of Income Dynamics (PSID) that took into account both incentives and benefits shows that work is significantly affected by incentives* (tax rates) and benefit levels (guarantees). They divided the states into four groups: low guarantee-low tax rate, low guarantee-high tax rate, high guarantee-low tax rate, and high guarantee-high tax rate, and correlated the annual hours worked by the female heads of poor families with these indicators of state welfare policy. While in the low guarantee-low tax rate states annual hours worked were 1,063 between 1967 and 1971, in the high guarantee-high tax rate states they were 598 or 40 percent less,[32] so that not only the decision to work but also the number of hours worked may be responsive to these program parameters.

The effects of high incentives and low benefits can be seen in the history of work effort in the southern states. Most of these states had their own work incentives long before 1967, that is, they paid only part of what the AFDC family "needed" and permitted working clients to keep earnings between the need standard and the payment standard without penalty. In addition, they paid extremely low benefits. Until 1967 the southern states had the highest proportion of AFDC mothers who worked. But between 1967 and 1977 in five southern states, the percentage decline in the segment of AFDC mothers that work ranged from 40 percent to 60 percent.

This radical decrease in work effort can be attributed to two factors: reduced work incentives and increased welfare benefits. The gaps between needs and payments that had permitted recipients to keep their earnings have narrowed considerably. Between 1967 and 1977, the percentage increase in the proportion of need that was paid varied from 20 percent to 196 percent, thereby substantially eroding work incentives in these states. At the same time, the percentage increase in the average monthly payment for a family of four ranged from 11 percent to 135 percent during these years. It is notable that Florida and Alabama, the two states with the greatest increases in benefits and reduction in incentives, showed the greatest decrease in work effort (Table 3.1).

In the south the thirty and one-third work incentive was tempered by the effects of reduced method-of-budgeting incentives and higher benefits. Since the national proportion of those that worked remained the same, it is probable that in states that had no previous incentives the new disregard increased work effort to some extent. However, as a national policy committed to increasing work effort, it could not compete

---

*A low tax rate is a high incentive, a high tax rate is a low incentive to work.

Table 3.1.
Percentage Change in Work Effort, Work Incentive, and Benefit in Five
Southern States, 1966–77

State	Work Effort	Work Incentive	Benefit
Florida	− 60	− 196	+ 135
Tennessee	− 47	− 21	+ 11
Mississippi	− 49	− 20	+ 47
Alabama	− 60	− 85	+ 99
South Carolina	− 47	− 50	+ 31

Sources: Derived from *Findings of the 1967 AFDC Study*, HEW, SRS, NCSS, Part I,
Table 38; Part II, Table 129; *1977 Recipient Characteristic Study*, HHS, SSA, ORS, Part I,
Table 25; Part II, Table 16, *Aid to Families with Dependent Children, Standards for Basic
Needs*, HEW, SSA, ORS, July 1977 and July 1967.

with decreasing incentives in the south and increasing benefit levels
throughout the country.

THE NEGATIVE INCOME TAX EXPERIMENTS

The thirty and one-third earnings disregard took place within the
parameters of the AFDC program and was instituted to encourage
AFDC family heads to work. The concept of a negative income tax
(NIT) was aimed essentially at the working poor and not the welfare
poor, was intended as the basis for a new income maintenance program to replace the AFDC program, and was concerned with the effect
of disincentives rather than incentives on work effort. In distinction to
the outright AFDC grant afforded to people selected because they are
impoverished, the NIT was to be targeted on everyone and attached to
the universal federal income tax system. Those whose income exceeded
a certain level would pay and those with incomes below that level would
receive payment. The intended effect of such an effort was to reduce
the stigma associated with the receipt of AFDC, to reduce the discretion
inherent in AFDC, to reduce state variations in AFDC policies and
benefit levels, and to be more "poverty-efficient" as it would also include the working poor. Unlike the AFDC program which is essentially
geared to female-headed families, the NIT would apply equally to families with a male head. Work incentives in the NIT, as well as guarantee
levels, would serve to insure that work effort among the working poor
continued.

The idea of a negative income tax was first circulated within the Office of Economic Opportunity (OEO) in the mid-1960s in what was

familiarly known as the poverty program. Economists attached to this program believed that the most efficacious way to reduce poverty was to provide income for those who lacked it. However, OEO was mandated to promote opportunity through community action and training programs and rejected the idea of solving the poverty problem through the direct transfer route. Within this context, these economists formed an effective lobby to promote the idea of a single national income-maintenance plan based on the concept of negative taxation. The Johnson administration seriously considered the proposal but decided instead to appoint the Heineman Commission to study the matter further. In the meantime, OEO, and later HEW, financed experiments to test the validity of the concept. The primary pragmatic question was whether such universal and unstigmatized aid would discourage work effort. It was important, then, to determine in advance what the effects of a negative income tax would be on the labor force participation of those already working. The critical variables were seen as the amount of the base income (the guarantee) to be received by those in need and the rate at which earned income was to reduce the guarantee (the tax rate).

For a decade between the late 1960s and the late 1970s, U.S. welfare policy was heavily influenced by the negative income tax ideology which was evident in the Nixon Family Assistance Plan in 1969 and the Carter Better Jobs and Income Program in 1977. Neither proposal became law, however, basically because the fear of labor force withdrawal persisted, among other reasons. The NIT was indeed a radical proposal that called for the transformation of the entire prevailing welfare system. As such it was not completely parallel to efforts to promote work within the AFDC program and differed in the following ways. As noted earlier, the experiments conducted around the NIT were concerned with disincentives to work rather than incentives, and were targeted on those already in the labor market rather than on those who were to be induced to increase their labor force participation. In addition, the new proposal attempted to institute a discretion-free impersonal system whereas, as documented in this chapter, work incentives in AFDC are based on substantial informal violations of statutory tax rates, thus considerably reducing tax rates. Finally, the benefits accrued from the current welfare system are not isolated from the benefits (and tax rates) of other means-tested programs such as Medicaid, food stamps, and housing allowances. Thus, the linkage between all of these programs results in extremely high formal cumulative tax rates for AFDC recipients.

Nevertheless, despite these divergent factors, the results of the NIT experiments do have some bearing on work incentives for the poor, regardless of the income-maintenance program that is in effect. Their findings therefore are of interest to us here. There were several of these experiments conducted with varying program parameters. We will, however, review only the Seattle-Denver experiment that took place from 1970 to 1978 since it used a sample that was 25 percent larger than the combined sample of all the other experiments, provided the most comprehensive information available on the question of labor force withdrawal, and included female heads. This experiment was applied to two groups of families: those that received payments for three years and those that received them for five years. The main findings were that the three-year group reduced their work effort by 7.6 percent among male heads, 16.7 percent in the wives group, and 13 percent among female heads. The five-year group had greater percentages of work reductions: 11.4 for husbands, 23.5 for wives, and 15 for female heads.[33]

The Seattle-Denver experiment clearly showed that work effort in all categories of recipients was substantially reduced under this kind of incentive plan. The lesson was learned here and applied in the BJIP that incentives need to be combined with job opportunities and work requirements in order to avoid voluntary decreases in work activity. Henry Aaron summarized these conclusions as follows:

> The findings on work effort, particularly those from the Seattle-Denver experiment, have led the administration to propose a welfare reform plan that unlike the simple negative income tax plan used in the experiment, integrates jobs and the reform of cash assistance. . . . All of the experiments provided guaranteed income maintenance payments but imposed no work requirements or provided no special job opportunities.[34]

The experiments helped to bury, probably for good, the concept of negative taxation as the means to a universal income subsidy program. Attention has now returned to the AFDC program as the focus of further efforts to promote work.

In summary, it would appear that the thirty and one-third earnings exemption did not have an appreciable effect on the work effort of AFDC mothers, especially when viewed from a national perspective. Some of the empirical studies cited above do show some increases in work effort, but apparently this resulted only when incentives were combined with low benefit levels. To offset the negative impact of rising benefits, incentives would need to be dramatically increased to produce a significant increase in work effort among AFDC mothers. Paradoxically, the Reagan administration appears to have forsaken the incentive strategy altogether, as we will see in the concluding chapter.

NOTES

1. Leonard J. Hausman, "Potential for Financial Self-Support Among AFDC and AFDC-UP Recipients," *Southern Economic Journal* 36, no. 1 (July 1969): 60–66, p. 60.

2. Genevieve W. Carter, "The Employment Potential of AFDC Mothers," *Welfare in Review* 6, no. 4 (July–August 1968): 1–11, p. 8.

3. Robert George Williams, *Public Assistance and Work Effort* (Princeton, New Jersey: Princeton University Press, 1975), p. 48.

4. Irene Lurie, "Estimates of Tax Rates in the AFDC Program," Institute for Research on Poverty Discussion Papers, No. 165–73 (Madison: University of Wisconsin, 1973), p. 22.

5. W. Joseph Heffernan, Jr., "Variations in Negative Tax Rates in Current Public Assistance Programs: An Example of Administrative Discretion," Institute for Research on Poverty Discussion Papers, No. 107–71 (Madison: University of Wisconsin, 1972), pp. 7 and 12.

6. Joel F. Handler and Ellen Jane Hollingsworth, "Work, Welfare and the Nixon Reform Proposals," *Stanford Law Review* 22, no. 5 (May 1970): 907–42, p. 927.

7. U.S. Department of Health and Human Services, SSA, ORS, *1977 Recipient Characteristics Study*, Part 2, "Financial Circumstances of AFDC Families," p. 35.

8. Michael J. Piore, "Income Maintenance and Labor Market Entry: The FAP Proposal and the AFDC Experience," *Poverty and Human Resources Abstracts* 5 (May–June 1970): 13–23, p. 13.

9. Handler and Hollingsworth, "Work, Welfare," p. 922.

10. N. A. Barr and R. E. Hall, "The Taxation of Earnings Under Public Assistance," Working Paper, Department of Economics, Massachusetts Institute of Technology, no. 85, April 1972, p. 19.

11. Lurie, "Estimates of Tax Rates," abstract.

12. Williams, *Public Assistance and Work Effort*, p. 51.

13. Alvin Schorr, "Problems in the ADC Program," *Social Work* 5, no. 2 (April 1960): 3–15, p. 9.

14. Carter, "The Employment Potential of AFDC Mothers," p. 9.

15. Irene Cox, "The Employment of Mothers as a Means of Family Support," *Welfare in Review* 8, no. 6 (November–December 1970): 9–17, p. 15.

16. Irwin Garfinkel and Larry L. Orr, "Welfare Policy and the Employment Rate of AFDC Mothers," *National Tax Journal* 27 (June 1974): 275–284, p. 283.

17. U.S. Department of Health, Education and Welfare, *Reasons for Opening and Closing Public Assistance Cases*, NCSS Report A-5 (July–December 1965, July–December 1966, July–December 1968).

18. U.S. Department of Health, Education and Welfare, *Reasons for Discontinuing Money Payments to Public Assistance Cases*, NCSS Report A-11 (July–September 1969, July–September 1970); U.S. Department of Health, Education and Welfare, *Applications and Case Dispositions for Public Assistance*, ORS Report A-12 (July–September 1977, July–September 1978, July–September 1979).

19. U.S. Department of Health, Education and Welfare, Welfare Administration, *Characteristics of Families Receiving Aid to Families with Dependent Children* (November–December 1961), Table 23; U.S. Department of Health, Education and Welfare, SRS, NCSS, *Findings of the 1967 AFDC Study*, Part I, "Demographic and Program Characteristics," Table 38.

20. U.S. Department of Health, Education and Welfare, SRS, NCSS, *Findings of the 1971 AFDC Study*, Part I, "Demographic and Program Characteristics," Table 21.

21. U.S. Department of Health, Education and Welfare, SRS, NCSS, *Findings of the 1973 AFDC Study*, Part I, "Demographic and Program Characteristics," p. 58.

22. U.S. Department of Health and Human Services, SSA, ORS, *1977 Recipient Characteristics Study*, Part I, "Demographic and Program Characteristics", p. 44.

23. U.S. Department of Health, Education and Welfare, SRS, NCSS, *Findings of the 1967 AFDC Study*, Part I, Tables 8, 40, 41, 55, Part II, Tables 97B, 99; U.S. Department of Health and Human Services, SRS, ORS, *1977 Recipient Characteristics Study*, Part I, Tables 1, 16, 28, 30, Part II, Tables 9A, 10.

24. *Economic Report of the President* (Washington, D.C.: Government Printing Office, 1979) p. 217.

25. Steve Erie, Gordon Fisher, Liz Dayan, "Preliminary Findings of the AFDC Population Study," U.S. Department of Health and Human Services, internal memorandum, December 3, 1980, p. 22.

26. U.S. Department of Health, Education and Welfare, *Effects of the Earnings Exemption Provision Upon the Work Response of AFDC Recipients*, Executive Summary, prepared by National Analysts, Inc., May 1972, p. 17.

27. *Effects of the Earnings Exemption*, pp. 21, 25.

28. Gary L. Appel and Robert E. Schlenker, "An Analysis of Michigan's Experience With Work Incentives," *Monthly Labor Review* 94, no. 9 (September 1971): 15–22, p. 18.

29. Gary L. Appel, *Effects of a Financial Incentive on AFDC Employment* (Minneapolis: Institute for Interdisciplinary Studies, 1972), p. 88.

30. *Characteristics of Families Receiving Aid to Families with Dependent Children* (November–December 1961), Table 23; *Findings of the 1967 AFDC Study*, Table 38; *Findings of the 1969 AFDC Study*, Table 19; *Findings of the 1971 AFDC Study*, Table 21.

31. *Characteristics of Families Receiving Aid to Families with Dependent Children* (November–December 1961), Table 50; *Findings of the 1967 AFDC Study*, Table 99; *Findings of the 1971 AFDC Study*, Table 56.

32. Barry L. Friedman and Leonard J. Hausman, *Work and Welfare Patterns in Low Income Families* (Waltham, Mass: Florence Heller School for Advanced Studies in Social Welfare, Brandeis University, January 1975), p. 86.

33. U.S. Congress, Senate, Committee on Finance, *Hearings Before the Subcommittee on Public Assistance*, 95th Cong., 2nd sess., November 15, 16, and 17, 1978 (Washington, D.C.: Government Printing Office, 1978), p. 9.

34. *Hearings Before the Subcommittee on Public Assistance*, p. 280.

4

Work Through Requirements

This chapter will examine work requirements as a strategy for reducing the welfare caseload. We view the WIN program as a work requirement for AFDC recipients that was not effective. There were several reasons for its ineffectiveness: it was torn by conflicting goals from its inception and throughout its history; the financing necessary for its implementation was unavailable; Congress was ambivalent about work requirements as social policy; and the professionals who were authorized to execute its provisions were ideologically opposed to the conception and able to translate this opposition into practice. Together these forces eroded the work requirement provisions of WIN. Four years after WIN's inception, Congress tried once again to reaffirm its belief in work requirements, but the same forces operated to undermine them, in practice. We will examine these processes and explore the implications of this experience for future work requirement policies.

In some states, especially the southern ones, statutory work requirements for AFDC mothers had been in effect since the start of the AFDC program. As late as 1967, 20 states had such requirements, many of which, however, were highly qualified and conditional and largely ineffective, judging by the small proportion of mothers at work.

With the advent of the Unemployed Parent segment of AFDC in 1961, work, in the form of Community Work and Training (CWT) programs, became mandatory for the unambiguously employable fathers that were brought into the program. The size of the UP rolls, however, remained small as did the CWT provision. Proposals for work requirements in the 1967 amendments to the Social Security Act sought to continue CWT, but Congress now had an additional agenda: work for AFDC mothers who headed the huge majority of AFDC families. The

WIN program was thus legislated as the first federally mandated effort to require all employable AFDC recipients to work or train for work.

This measure, in combination with the thirty and one-third disregard of earned income, was a response to the continuing growth of the AFDC caseload. Congressional anxiety is evident in the following excerpt from a report of the House Ways and Means Committee:

> Your committee is very deeply concerned that a large number of [AFDC] families have not achieved independence and self-support, and is very greatly concerned over the rapidly increasing costs to the taxpayers. Moreover, your committee is aware that growth in this program has received increasingly critical public attention.[1]

Work as a panacea for the "crisis in AFDC" reached its epitome in the 1967 amendments. These instituted the requirement that "all states establish a program for each appropriate AFDC adult and older child not attending school with a view to getting each of them equipped for work and placed on jobs."[2] The WIN program was to both train for work and refer to work all employable recipients.

But the WIN program, even from its conception in Congress, was beset by conflicting goals. The Committee on Ways and Means had recommended "the enactment of a series of amendments to carry out its firm intention of reducing the AFDC rolls by restoring more families to employment and self-reliance, thus reducing the Federal financial involvement in the program."[3] However, the amendment as passed also added the goal of creating "a sense of dignity, self-worth, and confidence which will flow from being recognized as a wage-earning member of society."[4] These two disparate functions—that of reducing the AFDC rolls and of enhancing the individual recipient's self-worth and competence—charged to WIN from the start, were instrumental in its lack of success.

The first mandate—reducing the AFDC rolls—could only be accomplished if large numbers of recipients were required to work; in effect, it meant establishing such a work requirement as a condition of eligibility. On the other hand, the goal of maximizing individual psychological and technical capability could best be achieved through rendering the individual a service. These conflicting conceptions of what the WIN program should be contain very different models. WIN as a work requirement calls for a program that draws a great many participants out of the recipient pool, that places them immediately in jobs or gives them directly work-related training, and that applies stringent sanctions to noncompliant behavior. The primary focus should be on job placement as quickly as possible for as many as possible. The contrasting paradigm, WIN as a service, would use a restrictive selection process, concentrate on training that is lengthy and not immediately work-related, seek to provide "career-ladder jobs," and make participation voluntary.

The conflict over whether WIN was a work requirement or a service continued in the implementation of the 1967 amendments and in practice. Although both conceptions were present, the HEW's classification of WIN as a service is symbolic of the tendency for that orientation to prevail. The program's evolution as a service can be attributed to both ideological and pragmatic forces. A work requirement entailed coercion, and the ambivalence inherent in AFDC over the advisability of forcing mothers to work persisted, in spite of the fact that mothers in the general population, even of very young children, were entering the labor market in increasing numbers.* There was also resistance to compelling fathers to work, so that it is evident that the reluctance to require mothers to work was imbedded in a distaste for coercion in general. Practical reasons for keeping WIN a service concerned cost. To train the multitude of recipients who could have been involved in the program, and to work toward creating jobs where they did not exist in the market, would have been exorbitantly expensive.

Both the conflict in goals and the ascendance of the service goal can be seen in three essential aspects of the WIN program: selection of participants, program components, and sanctions. Selection of recipients to participate in WIN was narrow and contrary to the broad mandate of the requirement that all appropriate adults be made ready for work. Program content in WIN was not directly job-related, and sanctions for noncompliance with WIN participation were not implemented. We will look at each of these dimensions as reflective of the erosion of the work requirement goal.

SELECTION OF PARTICIPANTS

If all adult recipients of AFDC were to be trained or employed through the WIN program, this would involve at least the 1,320,448 parents included in the 1,278,223 families on AFDC in 1967, not including the children over 16 years of age.[5] On April 30, 1970 the national total of authorized WIN slots was only 120,000;[6] clearly a way had to be found to eliminate over 1.2 million recipients from consideration for WIN. Congress took the first step in what was to be an ongoing

---

* "The steepest rise in work propensity has been among women with children under 3, whose labor force participation rate increased by three-quarters, from 15.3 percent in 1960 to 26.9 percent in 1972." *Manpower Report of the President*, March 1973, p. 66.

constriction policy by setting up categories of persons that the states would not be permitted to refer to WIN, and also specified the order of priority under which groups should be assessed and referred.

The federal legislative priorities formed a base for weeding out classes of recipients. The persons who could not be referred to WIN were the ill, incapacitated, aged, and those living too far away from a WIN project to participate; those attending school full-time; and those whose presence in the home was needed because of the illness or incapacity of another member of the household. However, in all cases a person requesting referral had to be referred unless the welfare agency determined that it was not in the best interests of the individual or the family.

As for priorities of referral and mandatory referral groups, preference was given in this order: unemployed fathers on AFDC-UP; children over 16 years who were neither at work nor in school; volunteer mothers with no preschool age children; and volunteer mothers with school age children. The only absolutely mandatory groups were the fathers and the children over 16 not attending school.

The federal guidelines to implement this legislation further stipulated that fathers and older children were the only groups that needed to be assessed for potential WIN eligibility. Since according to the law, child care services were to be supplied wherever necessary for WIN mothers, the guidelines stated that a recipient could not be referred if such services were not forthcoming. The guidelines also eliminated from WIN those mothers whose participation would endanger the family's well-being (a determination that the caseworker in the welfare agency was to make).

The states, however, were not prevented from adding still more qualifications. Massachusetts, for example, prohibited from involvement with WIN mothers of children under three years of age who did not voluntarily enroll. Sixteen states and Puerto Rico and the Virgin Islands made mandatory the referral of AFDC mothers "according to criteria specified by each state."[7] It is not clear what exactly those criteria were but it is clear that states were not referring groups of those mothers that they could consider essential referrals because of the "available child care" stipulation and the "family well-being" clauses of the federal guidelines. That these were operating criteria is evidenced by the fact that in 1969, of those not found appropriate for referral to WIN nationwide, 10 percent were ineligible because adequate child care arrangements were not available, while an additional 20 percent were "required in the home because of age or number of children."[8] By 1972 these figures were even higher—25 percent and 21 percent respectively.[9] Almost half of the assessments at this time were not referred to WIN for reasons of child care.

Caseworkers in local welfare agencies were still another force limiting the wide application of WIN. Since they made the "line" decisions regarding which of their clients were to be referred to WIN, their discretionary power in this matter was enormous. The Auerbach study clarifies this:

> The situation where a caseworker reviews all his cases in terms of a clear set of eligibility criteria for WIN, refers according to priorities . . . is almost non-existent . . . The effect is to make a fortuitous relationship between client and caseworker as much of a factor in screening and assessment as the guidelines and the eligibility requirements.[10]

Caseworkers, it will be remembered, were also responsible for deciding when participation in WIN was inimical to the family's well-being. The Massachusetts Department of Public Welfare considered a person inappropriate for referral to WIN "whose presence in the home is required because it has been determined *on a casework basis* that the continued absence of the person would adversely affect the well-being of a child. . . ."[11] (emphasis added)

Since caseworker discretion loomed large, their attitude in regard to employment was crucial. Handler and Hollingsworth, among others, have documented a negative view toward work for AFDC mothers and pointed out that it was basically a "social work decision" that was made jointly between the recipient and the caseworker about work. The decision was based mainly on familial and personal factors and was individualized, rather than made as an expression of welfare policy.[12]

As a result, according to the Auerbach corporation, "although each state has developed referral priorities in its guidelines, and most caseworkers have these guidelines at their disposal, priorities for other than mandatory unemployed fathers are not closely adhered to."[13] The usual procedure was that "the caseworker makes the mandatory referrals and then usually selects volunteers from among those he is currently in contact with."[14] According to caseworkers, "the most eligible candidates are those who are motivated, interested, young, able to secure childcare services, and have had at least some high school. Interest and motivation tend to be primary."[15]

Legislative priorities, federal guidelines, state limitations, and caseworker discretion had severely limited compulsory participation in WIN for AFDC mothers. Voluntary referrals took precedence in most states. Levitan, Rein, and Marwick note that "although participation has been made mandatory in some states for mothers with suitable child care arrangements, in most states mothers participate only voluntarily."[16] Evidence of voluntary participation is provided by the Reid and Smith study of 318 AFDC mothers in WIN, which notes that one-half of their respondents had initiated their own referral.[17] In fact, it was HEW policy as exemplified by the guidelines to discourage compulsory female participation: "It would be acceptable, and in fact desirable, for states to make referral voluntary for mothers of young children, and perhaps for those with older children who express a strong feeling that they are needed at home to take care of the children."[18]

All this had an effect on mothers' participation that was always heavily disproportionate to their prominence as heads of families in the AFDC program. During 1968, WIN's first year, only 46 percent of enrollees were mothers. By 1969, 58 percent were mothers[19] and by 1970 the figure was 71 percent.[20] Their degree of participation was also tied to how important it was at various times for fathers to use WIN. In 1971, the female proportion of enrollees dropped to 62 percent and by 1972 to 53 percent.[21] This occurred because the "unemployed parent" segment of AFDC, in which the father is present, doubled between 1969 and 1971 as a result of the economic recession. Mandatory referrals of men came first; whatever slots remained after that were accorded to mothers who were mainly volunteers. Since men and volunteers filled the limited slots available, the matter of compelling AFDC mothers to work never became an operative issue.

Reliance upon a principle of selectivity had the effect of diminishing the compulsory features of WIN, especially for AFDC mothers. Congress had legislated certain restrictions on its own dictum that all employable recipients should participate in WIN, by setting limitations on and priorities for referral. The federal guidelines interpreted the legislation in such a way as to even further narrow congressional qualifications. Some states, in turn, also delimited the WIN population, and caseworkers in local welfare agencies, through discretion in the referral process, desisted from involving mothers in the program. This funnel of selectivity comprising several levels of legislative decree and practical operation, narrowed to the end of eliminating compulsory work and training for AFDC mothers, who in 1969 headed over three-quarters of all AFDC families.

PROGRAM COMPONENTS

Another feature of the WIN program that illustrates the tension between work and training as a requirement and as a service, was its differentiated program components. Selectivity had factored employable recipients into priority-of-referral groups. Those AFDC mothers who made it through the selection process and became enrollees were further segmented or differentiated into job-readiness groups. Differentiation was based on the premise that the AFDC population was comprised of persons who were at different psychological and technical levels of readiness for work, a premise that derived, in turn, from the notion that *all* recipients were beset with formidable barriers to employment. The way to overcome these barriers was to "start where the client is" and create a program tailor-made to his or her individual needs. In order to achieve this complex goal, a giant superstructure replete with several subdivisions housing different components was erected. The end, presumably a job for each participant, was lost in the means—individualized training.

The number of such components was large. The first annual report of the DOL, the agency which in conjunction with HEW was responsible for the WIN operation, lists 13 program levels, any one of which an enrollee could presumably fit into at any given time, depending on his or her special needs. When a participant was "ready" for a higher level of training, he would be moved up. In addition, each enrollee, no matter at what point of job-readiness, had to go through a lengthy orientation period where he was introduced to the world of work and was made "aware of those attributes other than job skills required to obtain and hold a job."[22] Even those who were immediately employable received supportive services such as counseling for a minimum of 90 days, a directive of the DOL guidelines.

The WIN components can be clearly divided into two categories— those that were job-oriented such as vocational training, manpower training, on-the-job training, public sector employment, etc., and those that were not job-oriented such as orientation, prevocational training, general educational development, etc. Accounts of WIN have pointed out heavy concentration of WIN enrollees in the non-job-related components and much less participation in the others.

A report prepared by the DOL for Congress lists the number of enrollees in each component as of April 30, 1970: a full 60 percent of them were in the non-job-related components.[23] Reid and Smith reported that out of 124 female WIN enrollees they interviewed in three different cities, 48 percent were in educational courses (mostly high school) and only 14 percent in job-training courses; a full 35 percent were in "holding" (between components) status.[24] The Auerbach study similarly found that as many as 46 percent of enrollees were in basic education, only 25 percent were in institutional training, and another 25 percent were in prevocational or vocational training. Well over half were in the non-job-related components of basic education and prevocational training. Only 40 percent were sent to job interviews. It was concluded that "the more job-oriented the component, the less likely it is that the enrollee will be in it."[25] Franklin, in a California study of 360 enrollees, found that the WIN counselors expressed the opinion that 20 percent of their enrollees could have been immediately placed on jobs while another 36 percent "perhaps" could have been placed as soon as they entered.[26] Nevertheless, they were all processed through the WIN training components.

Structurally, much of the WIN program content was not job oriented. The results of this bias are clearly demonstrated by the outcomes of WIN participation. While the final goal for each enrollee was explicitly asserted to be a job, in fact, very few participants achieved it. As of December 1970, there were 23,691 people who successfully completed WIN (employed for from three to six months after obtaining a job); this was 10 percent of enrollees (and only one percent of assessed recipients). By April 1972, 61,500 out of 385,131 enrollees or only 15 percent were in this category.[27] Thus, a small proportion of enrollees obtained and kept jobs for a minimum of three months. How these jobs were procured is also significant. The Auerbach study revealed that only one-half of those who obtained jobs actually did this through WIN; the other half got their own jobs.[28] The kinds of jobs that WIN preferred for its enrollees may also have contributed to its lack of success in this area. WIN's avowed purpose was "training with a future" and "career-ladder" jobs.

Thus it is clear that program content in WIN sharply diverted the goal of work as a requirement even for its participants. It was geared to differential individualized treatment and each enrollee was "fitted" a program that was considered best suited to his or her needs and capabilities. Training was a lengthy and complicated process that assumed primacy over jobs. Program components emphasized non-job-related functions and enrollees spent more time in these subdivisions than in those that were directly work-related. The types of high level jobs in which WIN attempted to place its trainees were not consistent with the goal of providing work for many recipients.

SANCTIONS FOR NONCOMPLIANCE

Had WIN clearly represented a work requirement, it would have had to incorporate effective sanctions for noncompliance in order to enforce its norms. As it was, sanctions were mild in the legislation and rarely applied in practice. Congressional ambivalence was revealed at the outset when the WIN amendment, as passed, called for certain measures to be instituted against noncooperating recipients but tempered these measures in accordance with other concerns.

In contrast to the CWT sanctions which, in principle, penalized the entire family unit if the father refused work or training, in WIN only the individuals referred and not accepting referral, or in the program and refusing to continue, both without good cause, were to be deleted from the AFDC family budget. The assistance check would be reduced but not eliminated. In effect, the head of an AFDC household, though considered employable, was not constrained from not training for work or not working to support his family since the family would continue to receive AFDC support in any case.

But even the recalcitrant individual was not immediately denied an assistance grant. Removal from the rolls was only permitted after a sixty-day period of counseling by the welfare caseworker during which an attempt was made to persuade the recipient to comply. While this was happening, both the refusee and his family continued to receive the full assistance grant but it was paid to someone else as a "protective payment" and/or directly to vendors of food, rent, etc., instead of to the family. If after 60 days of counseling the referred person was still not willing to participate in WIN, he would be deleted from the budget but the family would continue to receive protective or vendor payments for as long as the case was otherwise eligible.

Some states even modified this procedure. Massachusetts, for example, had a 60-day period to allow the recipient to file an appeal against WIN referral which preceded the 60-day counseling period during which no punitive action was taken. There was, therefore, a 120-day grace period in all. In addition, great precaution was taken during the entire process to insure that the recipient was given every opportunity to comply and that there was indeed no good cause for him to refuse:

> Should the determination be made that an individual is appropriate for referral to the WIN program but refuses to accept referral, the social worker will further evaluate the recipient's suitability for referral, drawing upon the social study, and will reassess the recipient's motivation for participation in the program. In those cases in which referral is mandatory, the social worker will assist the recipient in working through his feelings about mandatory referral and explain to the recipient the penalties for refusal and notify the recipient in writing of his right to appeal such a determination.[29]

Not only were the legislative sanctions mild, but they were infrequently implemented in practice. The Auerbach report finds that sanctions were never really applied. Caseworkers said they did not have the time to do counseling and "the use of a protection and vendor payment is virtually unworkable." The report noted that "in most areas, including the largest urban areas, the number of applicants who had their benefits legally removed was a minute portion of those referred, despite the fact that thousands of de facto refusals had occurred."[30]

The GAO reported on the use of sanctions in Los Angeles and in

Denver. In Los Angeles, out of 107 fathers who refused to participate, the father's share of the welfare budget was discontinued in only 55 cases. In Denver no payments had been reduced through July 1970 although 94 fathers had refused to participate in WIN. California's county welfare departments said they "found the sanctions cumbersome and time-consuming for their limited staffs and imposed them on very few enrollees terminated from WIN without good cause."[31] Welfare agencies also were reluctant to apply sanctions because they saw them as resulting in hardship to the family.

Wherever sanctions were applied in this limited way they were applied to men. The GAO points out that in both California and Colorado, sanctions were only applicable to fathers. Goldstein, writing for the Joint Economic Committee, states "the penalty does not apply to mothers who volunteer for WIN. Since most of WIN's clientele are volunteer mothers, the sanctions are largely a fiction."[32] Levitan, Rein, and Marwick add:

> . . . in most states mothers participate only voluntarily, and therefore are free to leave without penalty . . . mothers constitute over half of WIN enrollment, but no sanctions are provided against most of them.[33]

Sanctions for noncompliance with WIN requirements were mild, infrequently used against fathers, and not applied at all in the case of mothers.

But what effect did this have on refusals to cooperate; were sanctions in fact necessary? Ten percent of referrals refused to participate. However, through June 1971 an additional 12 percent did not report for scheduled interviews and another 21 percent were turned back as either "unsuitable" or "unacceptable" with no reason given.[34] The actual proportion of referrals who were not enrolled because of refusal to participate without good cause may then be as high as 43 percent, or at least 22 percent. The other point in the WIN process at which sanctions were relevant was if the participant dropped out of the program after enrollment, again "without good cause." Of all enrollees "leaving before completion" through March 1970, 15.5 percent "refused to continue," 3.1 percent were "separated by administrative decision," and 6.5 percent "could not be located."[35] Thus, as many as 25 percent left WIN without good cause after having been enrolled. High refusal and dropout rates coupled with unenforced sanctions prevented the WIN program from functioning as a work requirement. This, combined with a highly restrictive selection process and program content that was not directly job-related, had the effect of narrowing WIN's success rate on all levels.

As a work requirement WIN should be judged on the basis of the number of recipients that it drew into the program and how many of these worked as a result of its training. On the first count WIN fell exceedingly short. Through fiscal year 1971, 2.7 million assessments had been made and only 24 percent of these were found by the welfare agencies to be "appropriate for a referral." Eighty percent of those deemed appropriate were actually referred, and less than three-fifths of these were enrolled. Enrollment on December 31, 1971, was only 118,000.[36] Throughout all program years, between 20 and 30 percent of terminees completed the program successfully, entered jobs, and were still working after 3 months. At each level of the WIN operation from assessment of recipients to job placement, the WIN funnel shrunk drastically. The result was a small program and a much smaller work success rate.

When we look at the case closing rate resulting from WIN participation, the numbers are even more telling. During hearings of the Senate Finance Committee in February 1972 it was noted that between July 1968 and December 1970, while there was a 1,169,000 increase in families receiving AFDC, there were only 20,000 AFDC cases closed following participation in WIN. The chart illustrating these data is pointedly titled: "The WIN Program Has Not Kept Pace with Increases in the Welfare Rolls."[37]

Even as a service, WIN cannot be judged to have been effective. The program did not lead to substantial increases in the job-obtaining and job-holding capacities of its enrollees. Only a small proportion of participants actually became involved in work as a result of contact with WIN. Auerbach Associates postulated that the "post-WIN employment behavior of WIN enrollees is nearly unaffected by participation in WIN. The dominant influences on the long-term employability of WIN enrollees appear to be the enrollees' initial capacity, their involvement with the low-wage, unstable labor market, and comparable value of welfare financial assistance."[38]

It should be remembered that congressional intent was to make it possible for every employable adult recipient to engage in work or training; the WIN funnel yielded only a trickle of this vast potential population. WIN then can be seen as a case of the failure of public policy to implement its own work requirements and a prototype of the difficulties encountered in this kind of endeavor. Perhaps the most important reason for this failure was Congress's own ambivalence. Both ideological and financial restraints compelled Congress to institute certain safeguards to insure that humane as well as economical considerations would be honored. The resulting tension between these goals and the predominance of the former defeated the primary objective of enforcing work requirements. An additional barrier to the actualization of these requirements was professional resistance. Although caseworkers in public assistance agencies were not themselves social work professionals, their stance regarding client rights and responsibilities derived from professional dictums that called for self-determination and disparaged coercion of any kind.

WIN II: THE TALMADGE AMENDMENT

In the midst of the deliberations and defeats of the various proposals for welfare reform, a proposal for amending the AFDC title of the Social Security Act "was added to an otherwise minor bill by the Senate during a sparsely attended session. . . . It was accepted today [December 14, 1971] by the House after virtually no debate."[39] This amendment, thereafter known as WIN II, was introduced by Senator Herman Talmadge. Its explicit purpose was "to improve the WIN operation," and it was essentially an attempt to strengthen the work requirement provisions of WIN. The first, 1967, WIN program had blatantly failed to accomplish its purpose of reducing the AFDC rolls and efforts to institute work requirements through the welfare reform proposals had also failed. Here was an opportunity, as some congressmen saw it, to effect a "get tough" stand on welfare without needing to evoke the opposition.

Essentially, the Talmadge amendment required that all able-bodied recipients register for work or work training. The aged, children under 16 or attending school, those caring for ill or incapacitated persons, and mothers of children under 6 years of age were exempted from this requirement. The federal government would match all WIN expenditures by 90 percent (as opposed to 80 percent for manpower training and 75 percent for supportive services in WIN I) and at least one-third of such expenditures had to be used for on-the-job training and public service employment.

There was great dissatisfaction in Congress with the selection process in WIN I whereby referral criteria were determined by individual states with widely differing outlooks. In addition, a great deal of discretion had been delegated by the states to the welfare agencies which, in turn, passed on a lot of their discretionary power to individual caseworkers. As a result, referral practices varied from state to state, from agency to agency, and even among caseworkers. Some states referred many recipients to WIN, others very few. It was felt that HEW, by encouraging the states to use "soft" referral practices, was responsible for the huge slippage between assessments and referrals since not only were referral rates varied but even more important, nationally they were low.

The counteract this and strengthen the selection process, the Talmadge amendment called for not the assessment of all recipients but for their registration if they did not fall into the excepted categories. Furthermore, since HEW and welfare were in disrepute, AFDC recipients were now to register directly with the DOL. To reward the states for sufficient referrals, the 90 percent matching clause was inserted; to sanction them for insufficient referrals, a penalty in the form of reduced federal assistance was to be levied if a state converted less than 15 percent of its registrations to certifications (enrollments).

The other feature of the Talmadge amendment to improve the selection of WIN participants was its dictum that volunteer mothers be accorded second place in the priority-of-referral scale with only mandated fathers coming before them. A number of studies had affirmed the willingness of AFDC mothers to work and it was the perception of some congressmen that in WIN, volunteer mothers had not been given enough attention and were kept waiting while mandated but not-so-willing participants (fathers and teenagers) "clogged" entry to the program. The poor success rates in WIN I were partly attributed to lack of motivation on the part of participants, so that maximizing volunteer participation should have the effect of maximizing job placements.

It had become increasingly evident that WIN I program content was not heavily job-oriented largely as a result of the influential Auerbach report, which recommended that there be more focus on job development, greater use of on-the-job training, and more extended use of special work projects. The Talmadge amendment accordingly specified that one-third of WIN funds be expended for on-the-job training and public service employment and also provided for a tax credit to employers who hired WIN enrollees, thus "reflecting a clear preference for real jobs as opposed to long-term classroom training."[40] It was hoped of course that this measure would lead to more, and more immediate, job placements.

Despite the GAO report noting that "the effectiveness of sanctions applied against persons who refuse to participate in WIN or to accept employment without good cause, appears questionable. Local officials have been hesitant to apply the sanctions . . .",[41] the Talmadge amendment did not alter WIN I's sanctions policy. Penalties for noncompliance by recipients were like those in WIN. After a 60-day counseling period, if the registrant was still not willing to work with the manpower agency, he or she was deducted from the AFDC budget while the family continued to receive a grant. If a recipient wished to contest the decision to remove him from the benefit schedule, he could "have a fair hearing process available at every step from appraisal to job referral."[42] Voluntary registrants could withdraw at any time without penalty.

The new legislation attempted to redefine some of the WIN features

that had prevented its success and had transformed it from a work requirement to a service program. Its innovations were primarily in the
areas of selection of participants and program content. To what extent
did these features actually change? The problem of under-referral was
structurally solved in the initial phase of the process. In WIN I, caseworkers in local welfare agencies made the starting assessments as to
who would be referred to WIN, while WIN II immediately registered all
recipients who did not fall into certain specified exempted categories.
In fiscal year 1973 there were 1.2 million such registrations; of these
511,000 were appraised as employable.[43] This last figure compares fa-
vorably with the 512,000 recipients deemed "appropriate for referral" in
the first two and one-half years (July 1968 to December 1970) of WIN I.[44]
Actual participants in WIN II during FY 1973 numbered 354,000[45] as
contrasted with the 118,000 enrolled in WIN I in December of 1971.
Under the new regulations the program immediately tripled in size. In
FY 1974 there were 353,900 new participants making a total for that
year of 534,900.[46]

Program content, in practice, was consistent with the new goal of
job placement (as opposed to job preparation). In 1973 there were
smaller proportions of WIN participants in "orientation," "skill
training," and "waiting" than there were in 1972. In 1973 there were 30
percent in "unsubsidized jobs" as contrasted with 16 percent in 1972
and 6 percent in "on-the-job training" and "public service employment"
in comparison to 4 percent in 1972.[47] In 1974 WIN was even more successful in implementing the job-placement goal. Participants in all of
the pre-job training components dropped from 52 percent in fiscal year
1972 to 12 percent in 1974. On-the-job training and public service
employment increased by 96 percent over the previous year, and the
number of recipients in unsubsidized employment was 30 percent
higher than in 1973.[48]

Although the Talmadge amendment made no significant changes
in the procedure for sanctioning those recipients who failed to comply
with WIN referral or WIN policies, in practice the WIN II operation
was more stringent than its predecessor. From July through December
1974, 8,180 WIN registrants received the 60-day counseling mandate as
a result of noncompliance, and 2,793 of them were "removed from
money payments" at the end of the period.[49]

In WIN II, more of the recipient pool became participants, program
content was more job-oriented, and more sanctions were implemented.
What effect did these reforms have on the usual measure of WIN success—job placements? In its first year WIN II recorded 137,000 job
placements, about 40 percent of participants. In a *four* year period,
WIN I had effected only 127,000.[50] Fiscal year 1974 saw as many as

177,300 job placements—as many as 50 percent of new (not all) participants.[51]

Undoubtedly, changes in the three program areas we have focused
on had the positive effect of increasing WIN II's volume of participants
and proportion of job placements. The selection process, for example,
not only registered more recipients, but also gave greater priority to
volunteers and those who were more employable. The latter policy
resulted in a population that was, as a whole, more amenable to successful participation. A study by Camil Associates of 4,700 "completed
job entries"—job placements in FY 1974—found that this group was
quite different from the general AFDC population: they were in their
prime working years, fairly well educated, had good work histories,
were in better health, and had been on welfare for relatively short periods. Both ability and willingness to work had an impact on program
outcomes.[52]

The condition of the labor market may have been another factor
that influenced results. From 1968 through 1971 WIN I operated in the
context of a rising unemployment rate. It was only in 1972 that unemployment dropped, a trend that continued in 1973. It can be argued that
during WIN II's first two years there were more jobs available. But
WIN's vulnerability to general labor market conditions becomes questionable when we examine the variations in performance within the
WIN I experience. Here, the number of enrollments increased each
year from 1969 on while the unemployment rate rose concomitantly.
This may have been due to the cumulative competence that the program achieved in time, which overcame the effects of the job market. It
is therefore difficult to assign a proper place to the labor market
variable.

Despite the improvements, WIN II, like WIN I, failed to achieve
either of the two goals that Congress had envisioned for it. The intent to
promote economic independence for AFDC recipients was thwarted by
the fate of the job placements that emerged from WIN. Of the 137,000
WIN participants in 1973 who entered jobs, only 65,000 (less than half)
were continuously employed for at least 90 days.[53] Smith, Fortune, and
Reid reported on a 1974 study of 121 former WIN participants in Chicago. This was a highly motivated, largely voluntary sample interviewed on an average of 18 months after leaving the program. The in-
vestigators found that 58 percent of the respondents were working but
half were on their second or third jobs. An additional 16 percent had
been working but no longer were. Most telling, 70 percent were still on
public assistance with 45 percent of these receiving benefits supplementary to earnings.[54] The national study by Camil Associates similarly
documents that only 42 percent of those cases where participants had

completed WIN and entered jobs were closed as a result, while the remainder received partial assistance from welfare.[55] Not all of those
removed from the welfare rolls were removed because of earnings that
met or exceeded the welfare benefit. Sixty percent of these successful
participants in 1973 were men, and the Unemployed-Parent provision
of AFDC forces male heads of families off the rolls when they work
more than 100 hours per month regardless of the level of earnings. In
summary, it is clear that many of those who had achieved job status
after or during WIN did not sustain it for long, changed jobs frequently,
and still remained on welfare.

As a service, WIN II also fell short. Camil Associates points out that
fewer than half of the "completed job entries" were placed by WIN, the
rest having obtained their own jobs before WIN training was finished.[56]
In the smaller study in Chicago, only 42 percent had obtained their jobs
through WIN. Also relevant is the fact that 90 percent of the respondents had previous work histories so that they were not strangers to the
labor market.[57] Camil Associates also examined wage levels for those
who had entered jobs: the difference in pre-WIN and post-WIN wage
rates was small, especially for those with previous work histories. They
concluded that "in general, WIN produced only a marginal impact on
those participants who obtained employment."[58]

It is clear that Congress intended WIN II—and WIN I—to put recipients to work and thereby make them economically independent of
welfare. Senator Carl Curtis's question when the bill was presented in
the Senate, "Is it not true that *the major objective* of the Talmadge
amendment was to get people on 'workfare' in contrast to 'welfare'?"
(emphasis added) was answered affirmatively by Senator Long.[59] Work
was to be the way to reduce the AFDC caseload in response to the
AFDC crisis. This would entail not only that large numbers of recipients be involved in WIN and placed on jobs, but that these jobs would
hold and keep people permanently off the rolls. Notwithstanding the
larger numbers of participants and placements that WIN II effected,
still only 13 percent of AFDC families had heads who were involved in
WIN in 1973,[60] and of these (as noted above) less than half were
employed for at least 90 days. The size of the caseload, understandably,
was not affected by the WIN program. In December 1972 there were
3,122,000 families on AFDC; in July 1974 there were 3,192,000; and in
July 1975, 3,475,000.[61]

Again, as in the former WIN program, ambivalence and financial
constraints prevented the execution of Congress's major aim. There
was ambivalence on all levels about requiring recipients to work. A
New York Times survey four months after the program went into operation pointed out that the Talmadge amendment had created "bitterness

and confusion" among the participating welfare and manpower offices and that,

> Officials of many welfare agencies simply do not believe in the concept of workfare and do not feel it will work. Some not only predicted failure of the program but indicated that they would attempt to defy implementation of the Talmadge amendment.[62]

Ambivalence in practice is reflected in the small proportion of "appraisals," compared with "registrations." In July 1974, for example, 66,100 recipients were registered, out of which as many as 51,400 subsequently became "deregistrations." Of these 51,400, 8,300 were employed, 13,500 were exempted, 2,300 refused to participate, and 27,200 (more than half) were in the category "other."[63] One wonders why those exempted were not exempted before registration in accordance with legislative priorities and what the significance is of the huge mysterious "other" designation. Annual figures tell the same story of the dwindling registrant pool. Such ambivalence had the effect of making WIN a requirement to register for work rather than a requirement to work.

Although there was a shift in WIN II away from lengthy and extensive training content, the greater volume of activity led to increasing program costs. Total WIN expenditures, including child care and other services, increased from $193 million in FY 1972 to $294 million in 1973 to $333 million in 1974.[64] These sums, however, were still insufficient to the task of incorporating the huge numbers of recipients that could have been involved in WIN. Despite the increases in cost, the WIN budget remained only a small part of the $2 billion annual funding cited by the Ways and Means Committee as the amount needed to fund a full-fledged reform effort.[65]

What might be called Congress's minor goal, that of providing a service to recipients by which they could upgrade their working skills through training, and achieve a higher standard of living, also remained unfulfilled. The median entry wage that successful job placements commanded in 1973 was $2.02 per hour—$2.58 for men and $1.87 for women.[66] In 1974 this wage was only slightly higher. The Chicago study found that the average annual net salary for men was $6,306 and for women $5,572. One-third of the men and two-thirds of the women involved needed supplementary assistance grants.[67] In short, earnings after participation in WIN were abysmally low.

But more important than wage levels was WIN's inability to affect the work pattern of most recipients in such a way as to help move them out of poverty. The Chicago study was useful in that it examined what happened to successful WIN completers on an average of 18 months later, thus making it possible to obtain longitudinal data. Certain impressions can be gleaned from these data about the group that "made it." They were people who had worked before and probably would have worked again even without involvement in the WIN program. They seemed to have had an erratic pattern of work that might be characterized as on again, off again accompanied by frequent job changes. They had low earnings which were often supplemented with welfare. Between jobs they may have depended on welfare exclusively. It is atypical for them to have been completely self-sustaining for long periods of time. These were the recipients for whom WIN did the most, yet even for them WIN did not change this pattern.

WIN III

In 1975 there were additional revisions in the WIN program, which at first developed largely through administrative regulations. Because this new initiative was more modest than the WIN II programmatic shift from institutional training to immediate job placement, it might better be described as WIN "two and one-half." Three new directions can be identified. First and perhaps most important was a new emphasis on the job search. This was based on the view that most of the unemployed manage to find jobs on their own, making use of personal contacts as well as formal channels. It seemed reasonable to apply the same logic to the employment of AFDC recipients.

Second was a recommitment to the WIN II legislation that called for cuts in institutional training expenditures and an increased emphasis on placing recipients in jobs through on-the-job training (OJT) and public service employment (PSE). Third, all new applicants to AFDC were required to simultaneously register with WIN as a condition for entitlement to AFDC. New welfare applicants were to be given "labor market exposure" (LME). That is, they were encouraged by an employment counselor to look for a job and were told about the importance of work. However, WIN had no authority to pay for any concrete service to the new applicant; WIN workers could only discuss employment opportunities but could not actively intervene to help place the new WIN enrollee in a job.

In 1980, amendments to the WIN legislation were passed through a rider to the Social Security Disability Act, and called WIN III.[68] These new amendments strengthen some of the above features in the WIN III redesign that were based on administrative guidelines rather than on legislative mandate. More specifically: WIN regulations permit the program to serve new welfare applicants, and free up resources to perform this function; individuals who are currently working will no longer have to register for WIN as they were formerly required by law to do; there is a return to a fixed sanction period of from 60 to 90 days, reversing a court decision to sanction recipients only for the time they refused to participate; and a four week job search is made mandatory.[69]

While WIN III is committed to finding and creating jobs for WIN recipients, at the same time it maintains an emphasis on what might be described as a programmatic balance. WIN's Tenth Annual Report to Congress observes that "experience has demonstrated that there is no typical WIN registrant and no best way that works for every registrant."[70] The emphasis on a "balanced program" arises from the recognition that WIN serves a heterogeneous population who require a wide range of services. Some WIN recipients have considerable work experience and can be helped through a job search to locate a job while others have very limited work experience and require job readiness programs. Still others are unable or unwilling for a variety of reasons to participate in the job and training program. As a result, it is necessary to have available opportunities for a front-end job search; for training programs of many kinds including skills training as well as language acquisition; for on-the-job training in the private sector; and for public service employment. The emphasis on balance is similar to the concern in the original WIN program with the differentiation of program components.

The attempt to achieve balance is also reflected in allocation formulas that call for both quantity—placing as many WIN recipients in jobs or training as possible—and quality—providing those who receive jobs with decent wages that will be sufficient to reduce the size of their welfare grants. Employment counselors are expected to be guided by a dual mandate: the need to reduce the welfare grant and increase the number of job placements per year. To achieve the first objective requires that the WIN recipient obtain a job that he will hold and that will be lucrative enough to have an impact on the size of the welfare grant. The latter objective emphasizes the quantity of placements. Funding restrictions may in fact create a tension between these two objectives. In the past five years, the funding for the WIN program has been remarkably stable at around $365,000 million.[71] However, the consumer price index rose quite sharply during this period of time. Thus stable funding has in effect meant a decrease of about 41 percent in the disposable resources available to WIN. In the 1981 budget the level of funding dropped to $354.8 million.[72]

THE WIN FUNNEL

Perhaps the strongest criticism of WIN II was its inability to solve the problem of the "WIN funnel," which reflected a strong selectivity bias leading to a discrepancy between AFDC recipients, WIN registrants, and actual job placements. The existence of the funnel was still evident from the most recent WIN statistics. Preliminary 1981 data show that there were approximately 3.5 million AFDC families of which 3.2 million lived in areas served by the WIN program. Out of this group came 1.2 million new WIN enrollees. This means that only about one-third of the total AFDC families qualified for the WIN program. Fourteen percent of all registrants were volunteers, that is, exempt individuals who elected to register. In addition to the new registrants, there were an additional 1.6 million WIN enrollees already on the books who were carried over from the previous year.[73]

During 1980, WIN revised its system of reporting. Under the new scheme, all registrants were divided into one of three categories: those who were assigned to a WIN component (defined as the program components provided directly by WIN); those who were assigned to a non-component category in which staff contact with WIN registrants amount to fewer than 12 hours per month; and those who were "unassigned" recipients.

The largest item in the WIN component category is Intensive Employment Services (IES). This is a programmatic activity designed to help WIN registrants spend at least 12 hours per week in the course of a job search. Approximately 196,000 or 53 percent of all WIN enrollees were assigned to this program. These statistics make it clear that the largest programmatic activity within WIN is the job search program. The job search procedure may be done in a very perfunctory way with the individual spending no more than a day or so in total looking for a job; alternatively, a considerable amount of demonstration initiative has been directed at creating a program in which enrollees spend at least six weeks looking for a job on a daily basis. Only some 40 WIN projects out of a total of 265 located throughout the country were involved in this kind of intensive group search effort.[74] The number of registrants involved in these projects was not available.

In addition to the IES program, which dominates all of the WIN activities, WIN recipients participate in the following program components in the numbers given:[75]

institutional training (provided directly by WIN)	30,000
on-the-job training	27,000
work experience	13,000
public service employment (provided directly by WIN)	9,000

| suspense to employment (CETA) | 66,000 |
| suspense to training (CETA) | 79,000 |

In the work experience component, the enrollee is expected to work for a state agency for a minimum of 13 weeks without any wages. The rationale behind the program is to provide work experience. It is designed specifically for those who have had no immediate or recent work experience.

Over a million participants fall into the "unassigned" category. In the past, this category was heterogeneous and included WIN registrants who had never been seen or contacted and those who had had contact once or twice. Currently, a new designation has been established called the "non-component" category. Those who have had any minimal contact with WIN personnel—largely to review their availability for work—are put in the non-component category. In 1980, it was estimated that 420,000 enrollees were so classified. What is important is that in both the unassigned group and the non-component group there is no involvement or only minimal involvement with WIN activities.

The WIN program, mandated to compel welfare recipients to work, seems to have evolved into a program that by 1980 primarily emphasized job search for about 200,000 persons; included a modest training, work experience, and jobs program run directly by WIN and serving about 80,000 persons; and had a much larger program of employment and training carried out by other programs, in particular CETA. Altogether, only about 100,000 slots are set aside for direct and indirect placement in a job: OJT, public service employment by WIN, and suspense to employment through CETA, which is based on the assumption that CETA would provide jobs for WIN recipients. Nevertheless, these various programmatic initiatives appear to lead to the placement of 280,000 individuals each year in full-time unsubsidized jobs that last at least 30 days or more. Approximately 10 percent of these participants do not continue in their jobs after 30 days.[76]

SANCTIONS

In 1980 there were 28,702 "notices of intent to deregister" an individual from the receipt of benefits. Only 50 percent of those who were notified were in fact deregistered: 14,401 individuals received such sanctions. It is estimated that in 1980 sanctions reduced benefits by $1.3 million.[77] Sanctions have never been widely employed by the states and litigations on sanctions further reduced their use. The courts had ruled that fixed sanctions were not legal, largely because of a mismatch between the time period of noncompliance with WIN requirements and

the sanctioning period. For example, a 10-day noncompliance produced a 60- to 90-day fixed sanction; the sanction did not "fit the crime."
As a result, in fiscal year 1980 and probably for a good portion of 1979
as well, most of the states made little use of sanctioning procedures
because of uncertainties regarding the courts' action. The new legislation in 1980 restored a fixed period of sanctions. It will be recalled that
the new sanction regulations, like the old, called for a reduction in the
grant of only the noncomplying member of the AFDC family. The remainder of the family continued to receive its grant. The rules again
called for a 60-day counseling period for the individual who is in noncompliance, followed by a letter of appeal, followed by a claims negoti-
ation where the final sanctions can be opposed. As we can see, there
are many safeguards for the individual in this procedure.[78]

WIN/WELFARE TAX CREDIT

The emphasis on immediate placement of current welfare recipients has been accompanied by an expansion of the special tax credit for
employers of WIN participants. The value of the tax credit called the
WIN/Welfare Tax Credit (W/WTC) was very generously increased in
1979. For employers in a business or trade, the credit is 50 percent of
the first year's wages up to $6,000 and 25 percent of second year wages
up to $6,000. The W/WTC also allows employers to claim credit for
hiring nonbusiness (household) workers for one year. In this case the
credit is limited to 35 percent of the first $6,000 paid to the individual
workers with a limit of $12,000 on total wages paid per employer.[79]

We know that almost 300,000 WIN enrollees were employed for 30
days or more in 1979 and only 42,713 of these were certified by WIN as
being entitled to enabling a tax credit.[80] WIN estimates that about 16
percent of working enrollees are certified for a tax credit. Under the
assumptions that an additional 20 percent are not eligible for these
credits because the firms in which they work do not qualify due to some
technical reason, and that an additional 10 percent do not work the 30
days that is required in order to be certified,[81]—it follows that about 55
percent of those who are employed in nonsubsidized jobs do not have
employers who claim a tax credit. This is of course very puzzling.

Two explanations have been proposed. The first is that firms essentially hire individuals on grounds other than the tax exemption to
which they are entitled; employers make a claim after they have hired
someone. Thus, the tax credit does not lead to new hirings but simply to
reimbursement after an independent hiring. By this logic, the tax credit

is largely ineffective because it compensates employers for hiring workers whom they would have hired on independent grounds. The second theory to account for why there are so few certifications for the tax credit among WIN registrants who are employed, is that many for-profit firms make no profit, and that many small firms and fly-by-night projects in which WIN recipients are employed fall into this category. It is estimated that as many as 40 percent of small firms might be classified as for-profit firms that make no profit during the year.

The tough policy of stressing work, sanctions, and incentives seems to have aborted in practice. WIN III placed its emphasis not on training, but on jobs, but, like its predecessors WIN I and WIN II, it produced a similar funnel effect—many registrants and few placements. The efforts to sanction clients for noncompliance remained more symbolic than substantive. And most disturbing was the curious inability to get employers who were entitled to tax credits for hiring welfare recipients to claim those credits.

CONCLUSIONS

With the passage of the 1967 amendments, Congress hoped to institute a work requirement for AFDC recipients in an effort to keep the growing AFDC rolls in check. The failure to achieve this goal compelled Congress in 1971 to again attempt to enforce work requirements, but in both instances professional and congressional ambivalence toward actions that might be considered coercive and limited financial appropriations diverted this aim.

Although both new WIN programs entailed somewhat more compulsion and effected more job placements, the proportion of participants to heads of recipient families was still extremely small and work neither persisted nor was sufficient to remove families from welfare. To accomplish the goal of reducing the caseload, many more participants would be required to enter the WIN program and many more to obtain and stay with higher paying jobs. Aside from the lack of a full commitment to the goal of work for all employable AFDC recipients, the primary obstacle was cost. Assuring work for earnings above the level of the welfare grant might entail work training, rather than educational and attitude training or job search, for a great many people and the active creation of a great many jobs. Both operations call for huge expenditures. A work requirement that requires people to work at jobs that yield less than the assistance payment, and that does not actually compel them to work, is bound to fail.

NOTES

1. U.S. Congress, House, Committee on Ways and Means, *Social Security Amendments of 1967*, 90th Cong., 1st sess., 1967, House Report on H.R. 12080.

2. Ibid., p. 96.

3. Ibid.

4. Stephen F. Gold, "The Failure of the Work Incentive (WIN) Program," *University of Pennsylvania Law Review* 119, Comment (January 1971), p. 487.

5. U.S. Department of Health, Education and Welfare, Social and Rehabilitation Service, *Findings of the 1967 AFDC Study*, Table 6.

6. U.S. Department of Labor and U.S. Department of Health, Education and Welfare, *Reports on the Work Incentive Program* (Washington, D.C., 1970), p. 78.

7. Ibid., p. 104.

8. Ibid., p. 180.

9. U.S. Department of Health, Education and Welfare, Assessments Completed and Referrals to Manpower Agencies by Welfare Agencies Under Work Incentive Program for AFDC Recipients (Washington, D.C., 1972), Table 5.

10. *Reports on the Work Incentive Program*, p. 246.

11. The Commonwealth of Massachusetts, Department of Public Welfare, *State Letter* 242, (October 1968).

12. Joel F. Handler and Ellen Jane Hollingsworth, *The Deserving Poor* (Chicago: Markham Publishing, 1971), Chap. 6.

13. *Reports on the Work Incentive Program*, p. 248.

14. Ibid., p. 246.

15. Ibid., p. 248.

16. Sar A. Levitan, Martin Rein, and David Marwick, *Work and Welfare Go Together* (Baltimore: Johns Hopkins University Press, 1972), first edition p. 96.

17. William J. Reid and Audrey D. Smith, "AFDC Mothers View the Work Incentive Program," *Social Service Review*, 46, no. 3 (September 1972): 351.

18. *Reports on the Work Incentive Program*, p. 229.

19. Ibid., p. 176.

20. Levitan, Rein, and Marwick, *Work and Welfare*, p. 79.

21. Ibid., and *Assessments Completed*, Table 3.

22. Vernon K. Smith and Ayden Ulusan, *The Employment of AFDC Recipients in Michigan*, Michigan Department of Social Services (1972), p. 29.

23. *Reports on the Work Incentive Program*, p. 76.

24. Reid and Smith, "AFDC Mothers," p. 356.

25. Auerbach Associates, *An Impact Evaluation of the Work Incentive Program*, Volume I (Philadelphia, 1972), p. I-8.

26. David S. Franklin, *A Longitudinal Study of WIN Dropouts: Program and Policy Implications* (Los Angeles: Regional Research Institute in Social Welfare, 1972), p. 8.

27. Jon H. Goldstein, *The Effectiveness of Manpower Training Programs: A Review of Research on the Impact on the Poor*, Studies in Public Welfare, Paper no. 3, U.S. Congress, Joint Economic Committee, 1972, p. 52.

28. Auerbach Associates, *An Impact Evaluation*, pp. 1–15.

29. *State Letter* 242, p. 5.

30. *Reports on the Work Incentive Program*, p. 260.

31. U.S. General Accounting Office, *Problems in Accomplishing Objectives of the Work Incentive Program*, 1971, p. 23.

32. Goldstein, *The Effectiveness*, p. 51.

33. Levitan, Rein, and Marwick, *Work and Welfare*, p. 96.

34. Ibid., p. 95.

35. *Reports on the Work Incentive Program*, p. 39.

36. Levitan, Rein, and Marwick, *Work and Welfare*, pp. 93, 94, 99; U.S. Senate, Hearings, Committee on Finance, *Establishing Priorities Among Programs Aiding the Poor*, 92nd Cong., 2d sess., 1972, p. 78.

37. Ibid., p. 74.

38. Auerbach Associates, *An Impact Evaluation*.

39. *New York Times*, December 15, 1971, p. 42.

40. Office of Management and Budget, "Federal Income Security Programs," from *Special Analyses, Budget of the U.S. Government, 1973*, January 1972, p. 185.

41. *Problems in Accomplishing Objectives of the Work Incentive Program*, p. 2.

42. U.S. Department of Labor, *Manpower Report of the President*, 1973, p. 39.

43. U.S. Department of Labor and U.S. Department of Health, Education and Welfare, *Manpower Report of the President*, 1974, p. 132.

44. Goldstein, *The Effectiveness*, p. 52.

45. *Manpower Report*, 1974, p. 132.

46. U.S. Department of Labor and U.S. Department of Health, Education and Welfare, *Manpower Report of the President*, 1975, p. 107.

47. *Manpower Report*, 1974, p. 132.

48. *Manpower Report*, 1975, p. 109.

49. U.S. Department of Health, Education and Welfare, Social and Rehabilitation Service, *Work Incentive Program December 1974*, 1975, p. 20.

50. *Manpower Report*, 1974, p. 132.

51. *Manpower Report*, 1975, p. 107.

52. U.S. Department of Labor, *A Retrospective Case Review of WIN-II Completed Job Entries: Grant Reductions, Services, and Welfare Savings*, prepared by Camil Associates, Philadelphia, 1974, pp. 2–4 and 2–5.

53. *Manpower Report*, 1974, p. 132.

54. Audrey D. Smith, Anne E. Fortune, and William J. Reid, "WIN, Work, and Welfare," *Social Service Review* 49, no. 3 (September 1975): pp. 398–400.

55. *A Retrospective Case Review*, p. 2–2.

56. Ibid., pp. 2–5.

57. Smith, Fortune, and Reid, "WIN, Work and Welfare," pp. 399, 400.

58. *A Retrospective Case Review*, p. 2–5.

59. U.S. Senate, *Congressional Record* 117, no. 196 December 14, 1971, p. S21646.

60. U.S. Department of Health, Education and Welfare, Social and Rehabilitation Service, National Center for Social Statistics, *Findings of the 1973 AFDC Study*, Part I, Table 51.

61. U.S. Department of Health, Education and Welfare, Social Security Administration, *Social Security Bulletin* 39, no. 1 (January 1976): p. 70.

62. *New York Times*, October 9, 1972, p. 46.

63. U.S. Department of Health, Education and Welfare, Social and Rehabilitation Service, *Work Incentive Program, September 1974*, 1975, p. 2.

64. Levitan, Rein, and Marwick, *Work and Welfare* (third edition), Postscript.

65. Levitan, Rein, and Marwick, *Work and Welfare* (second edition), Postscript.

66. *Manpower Report*, 1974, p. 132.

67. Smith, Fortune, and Reid, "WIN, Work, and Welfare," p. 400.

68. *Social Security Disability Amendments of 1980*, Public Law 96–265, Section 401, "Amendments on the Social Security Act."

69. U.S. Department of Health, Education and Welfare, Office of Human Development Services, *Federal Register*, Part XII, April 22, 1980, pp. 27420–27423.

70. U.S. Department of Labor, Office of the Secretary, WIN: 10th Annual Report to Congress, December 19, 1980, p. 3.

71. Ibid., p. 23.

72. Data are based on the Continuing Budgetary Resolution of Congress. The funding level continued until March 30, 1982.

73. U.S. Department of Labor, "WIN Program: Management Information Report," (unpublished) September 30, 1981, Table D-1.

74. Correspondence with Nancy Snyder, Acting Executive Director, National Coordinating Committee, Work Incentive Program, Department of Labor and Department of Health, Education and Welfare, March 26, 1981.

75. These data were made available in personal correspondence with Bob Easley, Unit Chief, Division of Program Design, Work Incentive Program, U.S. Department of Labor, April 1981.

76. All of the above WIN statistics come from "Employment Security Automated Reporting System, National Report," Department of Labor, Employment and Training Administration, Table 33, Item 33140, September 30, 1980.

77. Department of Labor, "Selecting WIN Activity by Characteristic of National Report, Table 30, Period ending September 30, 1980, p. 001.

78. Department of Labor, Office of the Secretary, Federal Register, Part XI, (April 22, 1980), p. 27414.

79. Ibid.

80. U.S. Department of Labor and the U.S. Department of Health and Human Services, WIN: 10th Annual Report to the Congress, The Work Incentive Program (December 1980), p. 15.

81. Personal correspondence with Bob Easley.

5
Work and Welfare Patterns: Qualitative Analysis

In the preceding chapters we noted the dramatic rise in AFDC costs and caseloads and examined the reasons for these increases. We then looked at three policy initiatives instituted in response to the rise, all of which aimed to promote work among AFDC family heads. The assumptions inherent in these work strategies were that welfare mothers are not able to work and therefore need services to effect this goal; that welfare mothers do not want to work and consequently need incentives to encourage them to do so; and that welfare mothers are not willing to work and need work requirements to so compel them. Underlying these assumptions were the beliefs that AFDC family heads in fact do not work and that their almost exclusive source of income is welfare.

Such beliefs stemmed from information reported in the official biennial AFDC surveys which indicate that only 14 to 16 percent of these mothers work during any one month.[1] The picture of work activity in AFDC derived from these surveys and incorporated by policy-makers is one that portrays the AFDC basic population as essentially a non-working group that is totally dependent upon welfare. However, other quantitative analyses that take the longer time period of a year into account have found that a much larger proportion of welfare family heads work.[2] And qualitative studies of inner-city areas[3] have illustrated that rather than having only one source of income such as work or welfare, these urban families have many sources—cash and in-kind, formal and informal—that form a composite income package that changes frequently over time.

To obtain a better understanding of the relevance and efficacy of the work policies instituted by government in the mid-sixties and 1970s, we attempted to question the assumptions that informed them, and, by doing so, to examine the work actually performed by recipients and the variety and stability of the total income package. More specifically, we wanted to know to what extent work is undertaken and under what conditions; who in the family unit works; how continuous that work is; what level of living it affords; and what its relationship to other income sources—especially to welfare—is. We were also interested in the remaining income sources such as welfare and food stamps, the work-related benefits such as social security and unemployment compensation, and private transfers—child support, free rent, and help from friends and relatives.

In regard to the total income package, we wanted to know how complex it is, how many components it comprises, how much each contributes to the total, and how stable the package is. We were interested in how income sources are related to each other and to personal and family characteristics and styles of life.

In order to answer these questions, a segment of the welfare-risk population was selected: the women and their families who live in the center-cities of large metropolitan areas. This groups represents a sizeable portion of the national AFDC caseload, is seen by policy-makers as an intractable aspect of the "welfare problem," and, because of residential concentration, may reflect a "welfare culture."* Six hundred forty-two thousand, almost 20 percent of all AFDC families, live in the largest central cities of one million or more inhabitants, while another four hundred nineteen thousand—or almost half a million—live in cities of from one-half million to one million residents.[4] U.S. census data tell us that of the poor female-headed families with children who receive public assistance income, 67 percent live in the poverty tracts of low-income areas in large cities.[5] Furthermore, employment opportunities are more prevalent in urban areas.

The policy interest in poor female-headed families who live in neighborhoods where there is a concentration of such families and where welfare use is high was first publicized by Bradley Buell and Associates in 1951 when it was discovered that the bulk of a city's resources were being spent on a very small group of poor families.[6] More recently, a review of the official biennial AFDC surveys revealed that the long-term receipt of AFDC (four or more years continuously since most recent opening) was more prevalent in the metropolitan areas of large cities than elsewhere in the country, and that this trend is growing.[7] To add to this account, a Rainwater and Rein analysis of the

---

*Barbara Boland documents that in 1967 and 1970, female-headed families living in northeastern and western central cities had higher AFDC participation rates than other groups (see Note #14, Chapter 1).

PSID data indicates that almost two-thirds of all welfare income is absorbed by those who have been on welfare for a continuous five-year period.[8] As welfare costs have increased, so has the concern for the convergence of expenditures upon families clustered in urban areas—one facet of the recent preoccupation with the "overload" of the modern welfare state. The high visibility of such families given their state of poverty and concomitant area residence, has further exacerbated the problem and resulted in allegations of intergenerational dependency and a theory of a "culture of poverty."

To capture the welfare-risk, center-city population of interest here, 206 families were chosen with the following characteristics: they were living 15 or fewer miles from the center of a city of 50,000 or more in one of 12 urbanized states;[9] they were female-headed in at least one of the ten years from 1968 to 1977; they had a child or children under 18 years of age; and they had received $299 or more of welfare income in at least one of the ten years. In short, these were the ever-welfare, ever-female-headed families with children who lived in the center-cities of large metropolitan areas.

The data base from which this analysis of the income sources of this population was derived is the Panel Study on Income Dynamics (PSID), an annual survey dating from 1968 and still being conducted of 5,000 families by the Institute for Social Research at the University of Michigan. This is a national sample oversampled for low income respondents that focuses on income sources and related variables. Thus it is uniquely appropriate for the analysis undertaken here. Many scholars have used the PSID survey to compile income and corollary data, but none to date have focused on the inner-city welfare population.

We have examined PSID data by two methods: quantitative and qualitative. The quantitative analysis uses the 206 families discussed above, 91 of which were female-headed throughout the ten year period from 1968 to 1977 and 115 of whom changed their marital status during these years. The women in the latter group were married in at least one of the ten years and were single, divorced, or separated in at least one other of the ten years.* The chapter following this one analyzes these 206 families quantitatively in the aggregate and also dichotomizes them by welfare status and race. For the qualitative analysis in this chapter, 30 cases were selected at random from the 206; 15 from the always-

---

*Widows were not included because it was felt that their work, welfare, and other income sources would be quite different and less typical of this subpopulation than those of the single, divorced, or separated women. The women in both our categories were between 18 and 54 years of age.

female-headed group and 15 from the "changed-status" group to produce a viable data base.

Essentially the same research questions are asked of the quantitative and qualitative analysis; as noted before, these are concerned with the nature and extent of work performed, and the composition of the total income package. The quantitative effort, however, focuses only on income variables while the qualitative examination also includes personal characteristics, family structure and household composition, and employment behavior. The purpose of the qualitative analysis then is to relate income-maintenance patterns to the lifestyles of these families, the contention being that such patterns are determinant of and intricately intertwined with total living patterns.

Specifically, the qualitative investigation is concerned with the processes by which income is acquired, the transition points between changes in sources and levels of income, and the interaction between events that produce specific income variations. Thus, the factors that impinge upon work, welfare, and other income decisions can be isolated.

The qualitative analysis of the 30 cases used the methodology of "print cases"—that of printing out specific variables on each individual case over a ten year period. Thus, each cash situation in its entirety could be seen at a glance. Such a method is sometimes employed to detect errors in survey data but was used here for the quite different purpose of creating access to the complete, longitudinal, and detailed picture of an individual family over an extended time period.

This unique method of analyzing survey data qualitatively permitted us to obtain a continuous, holistic account of the income sources and other characteristics of these families that could otherwise be achieved only through more open-ended field work techniques. However, data retrieved through field research methods are impressionistic and therefore not as precise as survey data. On the other hand, quantitative data analyzed in the aggregate, as is usual, can neither tap the processes that lead to certain decisions nor ascertain the relationship between variables.

This method would seem able to avoid these pitfalls, but it has limitations of its own. Some portion of these data were not internally consistent, undoubtedly due to error that in quantitative analysis is assumed to be random and is ignored. In other cases, the "stories" that the data told were not absolutely clear in that events could not be related to each other in a meaningful fashion.* Unfortunately, we did not

---

*These problems with the methodology proved quite substantial in six cases, one "always-female-headed" family and five "changed-status" families which had to be eliminated from the analysis because a consistent story could not be obtained from the data. This left 14 always-female-headed and ten changed-status families in the final sample.

have access to the actual interview schedules located at the University of Michigan; these are replete with interviewer comments that would have provided the missing links. We therefore had to "read" the cases by partly relying on intuitive judgments that were based on previous experience.* However, in spite of these limitations, the analysis afforded a surprisingly rich and comprehensive picture of how these families made work and welfare decisions and packaged income.

To obtain such a holistic account for the qualitative analysis, 54 variables[10] were run for each case for ten years, and consisted of income sources (work, welfare, and other sources), employment behavior, family structure and household composition, and personal characteristics. The purpose was to relate the income package to familial and social factors and events in order to elucidate 1) types of work and welfare income packages; 2) transition points between work and welfare decisions; and 3) the levels and stability of income packages.

TYPES OF WORK AND WELFARE INCOME PACKAGES

The 24 cases involved in the survey fell into three types of income packages. Type one, "welfare career" families, involved little or no woman's labor with AFDC being the sole source of basic income. In type two, "welfare primary" families, there was some work by the woman, but AFDC was the primary source of income; work was used to supplement welfare. By contrast, the "work primary" type three included those families where work was performed by the woman either continuously or almost continuously and was the basic income source while AFDC was used to supplement work. These work and welfare patterns will be correlated with other income sources and life events so that the context from which work and welfare decisions are made will be clarified.

Type One: Welfare Career

The welfare career type predominated in the always-female-headed cases and was also present to a lesser degree in the changed-status families. (There were eight always-female-headed and two changed-status families in this type.) AFDC was received every year while work for the female head was either nonexistent or took place during one or two years with very little income resulting from it. When work did take

---

*The author has worked for eight years in settings where welfare recipients were agency clients.

place, it was invariably domestic work. The other major income source was food stamps, which were also received every year along with AFDC. AFDC and food stamps were usually supplemented by small amounts of income derived from the work of older children, "income from other source" (help from friends), occasional help from relatives and, in some cases, child support from an ex-husband.

Age, race, education, and the number of children were not significant in that they varied a great deal in these families. Some other attributes, however, were highly typical. For example, domestic work was always the occupation given. In many instances, no work income was declared although this occupation was listed and a paid baby sitter was used to care for small children. It is conceivable that more of such work was done than was acknowledged. In many cases, disability was claimed by the woman.

Family dynamics were such that children were often born every few years even while the woman was separated, divorced, or single. No legal husbands were visible but the presence of a boyfriend either living in the family unit or outside was signalled by "income from other sources" or a designation of the woman living with "unrelated others." In a very few instances, child support payments from a previous legal husband or other father were acknowledged. In changed-status cases, a woman was often married with the male head's labor income considerably high, but with substantial AFDC income at the same time. It can be assumed that these were stepfather cases where the new husband was not legally responsible for the support of children from a former husband. Another theme was older children having some earnings for a few years, then leaving the household (they may in fact have left because their earnings jeopardized AFDC eligibility). In any case, children's labor income was not a source that could be depended on indefinitely. Still another theme was the tendency for such families to live with either related or unrelated "others." This was especially prevalent in always-female-headed families where the unit was comprised of the woman, her children, siblings of the female head, grandchildren, nieces and nephews, parents, boyfriends, or total strangers. These "others" often had earnings and transfer income of their own and at minimum, probably shared in paying rent and utilities. They generally did not stay long, however, and moved in and out frequently.

One simple example of the welfare career type is Mrs. A who was black, a high school graduate, aged 42 in 1968, and "separated" all ten years. The family unit consisted of a woman and her three children, the youngest of whom was seven in 1968 and the oldest 16. A one-year-old grandchild was brought into the household in 1969 and stayed throughout. Eventually all three of Mrs. A's children moved out, with one moving back in the last of the ten years.

Mrs. A. listed no occupation, but her small grandchild was in a day care center in 1972. She claimed total disability some years, a little disability some years, and no disability other years. Mrs. A. acknowledged no earnings of her own. The major source of income in this family was AFDC every year, which was received for the grandchild when Mrs. A.'s own children moved out. A secondary income source was food stamps that were received for the last seven years. The older children worked and this inflated the unit's total income while they were present, although the AFDC grant was reduced accordingly until they moved out when it was increased again. Another small source acknowledged for one year was reported under "income from other sources" and may have been the contribution of a boyfriend.* Thus, Mrs. A. declared no work income; her basic income package was comprised of AFDC, food stamps, children's earnings, and a little outside help, probably from a boyfriend.

A more complex example of the welfare career type is the case of Mrs. B., a white woman aged 30 in 1968 with an educational background of grades nine through eleven† who gave her marital status as single throughout. Mrs. B. had two young children in 1968, but gave birth to a third child in 1969 and a fourth in 1972. An unrelated person moved in in 1971 and moved out in 1975. This appeared to be a man with whom Mrs. B. was living and the father of her two new children.

Mrs. B. did domestic work in 1970 and 1971 for only 250 and 480 hours respectively. She paid for child care these two years and reported that her child or children were also in a day care center in 1972 with no work acknowledged for this year. The major source of income, however, was AFDC every year, supplemented by food stamps the last four years. An additional substantial income source was child support every year but one, which was from the father or fathers of the two oldest children. Beyond this, the unrelated person in the household showed earnings for three of the five years that he was resident and also received an unspecified source of transfer income for two of these years.

This family's income package consisted primarily of AFDC every year, then food stamps, child support from a previous father, the small

---

*Susan Anderson-Khleif did a content analysis of female-headed welfare families' interview schedules in the PSID survey and found that the variable "income from other sources" frequently denotes economic aid from boyfriends.[11]

†Educational level is a categorical variable in the PSID data and there covers three grades.

earnings of Mrs. B. for two years, and the labor and transfer income of the unrelated person with whom she was living. It seems likely that Mrs. B also had additional income from her own domestic work, which was not acknowledged.*

Type Two: Welfare Primary

In type two, welfare primary families—of which there were one always-female-headed and four that changed marital status—AFDC was still the basic source of income but to a fair degree it was supplemented by work. This was performed by the woman during three to six out of the ten years, and typically was acknowledged to be for only a few hundred hours in each of those years. AFDC and food stamps were received every year right along with the smaller work income.

Family structure in the changed-status cases of this type changed a great deal. Very often more than two marriages or other such liaisons took place within the ten-year period, with separations between. When new husbands came onto the scene, AFDC was reduced if the male head was employed, but continued nevertheless because these men were not legally responsible for the support of previous children. If male heads were unemployed, the family received either AFDC-UP or GA. As in the case of welfare career families, the residential unit often included related or unrelated persons, especially when it was female-headed. Older children in these families also worked for a few years and then left, with some returning.

Income sources other than work and welfare were child support from a previous husband, children's earnings, help from relatives, "income from other sources," and expense sharing and/or assistance from related and unrelated persons in the household. In addition, as in welfare career families, there were some indications that income from domestic work may have been underreported.

A very typical example of the welfare primary type is Mrs. C., who is black, aged 33 in 1968, and had an education of grades nine to eleven. Her family unit received AFDC all ten years and food stamps for eight of the ten years. She worked as a domestic for three nonconsecutive

---

*Anderson-Khleif's analysis reveals that "women who work as domestics in private homes . . . [often] do not report their real full salary and also receive all sorts of help in kind through association with the wealthier household . . ." This is because acknowledging all money income is not feasible in the advent of welfare receipt, and in-kind help is difficult to translate into dollars.[12] Some "flags" in the data for this underreporting of work income are child care expenditures and the listing of occupations in years when no earnings are acknowledged.

years for a maximum of 780 hours in one of the three, and as a machine operator one year 40 hours and another year 310 hours. Her primary and continuous income base, however, was AFDC.

Mrs. C. was divorced in 1968, remarried for two years, then separated for six years, and remarried again. It is not at all clear whether these last two unions were legal marriages; no new children were born of them. She had four children in 1968 from her first husband, two of whom eventually moved out. Mrs. C. lived with her father or mother until the second male head moved in in 1969 at which point this parent moved out.

Both her second and third husbands worked and had fairly high earnings when present. Mrs. C. worked during one of the years that she was with her second husband, for three years while separated, and for one year while with her third husband. AFDC continued throughout because neither man was legally responsible for her children. Since her work netted her low earnings, AFDC supplemented and superceded her work income. Other sources of income were child support from her first (and possibly only legal) husband for five nonconsecutive years, children's earnings, and help from relatives for one year. This family's income package, which consisted primarily of AFDC and food stamps, stemmed from the same income sources whether Mrs. C. had a husband or not. The male heads' earnings simply became an additional source resulting in reduced AFDC and food stamps grants but not eliminating them.

Type Three: Work Primary

Type three, work primary—of which there are five always-female-headed and four changed-status families—consisted of women who had worked every year or most years, and worked sufficient hours to derive their basic income from this source. AFDC may have been used continuously to supplement earnings, or it may have been received sporadically when labor income was reduced or nonexistent.

The characteristics of the work primary group differed markedly from the welfare career and welfare primary types. While the number and ages of children varied here as they did in the others, and older children worked and then moved out, other aspects of family and household structure were not the same. In the changed-status cases, for example, marital status (when not married) was always divorced, rather than separated or single. In contrast to the other type groups, there was never more than one remarriage. Typically, the always-female-headed women were divorced. In addition, there were no families of this type that lived with unrelated others although many lived with related persons. The residential unit therefore was more likely than in the other two types to be either nuclear or nuclear-plus-related.

These women's labor income was not only greater due to more work hours, but also because they tended to earn a higher hourly wage. This is at least partly explained by the mix of occupations that they engaged in—domestic, clerical/sales, and professional/technical—as contrasted with only domestic work in the other groups. The woman's work here took several forms. It continued throughout the ten years regardless of whether a marriage took place, or it ceased when a woman formed a new liaison with a man, or it stopped or started when a marriage ended. When a husband was present, his earnings too were uniformly higher than husbands' earnings in the other type groups.

In these work primary families, income from AFDC not only formed a smaller proportion of total income, it was also more tied to other factors. For example, AFDC as a source and level of income depended heavily on the woman's labor income. When work stopped or started or when earnings went up or down, AFDC fluctuated accordingly. Food stamps, which generally accompanied AFDC, also varied for the same reasons. In some instances, full AFDC was obtained initially when there was no work income, then partial AFDC when earnings rose, then no AFDC as labor income increased even further. In most cases, however, both labor and AFDC income fluctuated together unevenly throughout the years. Unlike in the other groups, the receipt of AFDC here was also sharply affected by the presence of a husband, at which time it ceased to be a source of income.

Other sources of income in the work primary families were, as with the other types, children's earnings, child support from a previous husband, and some income from other sources (presumed to be a contribution from a man living outside the household). Here, however, living with related persons, very often a mother or father of the female head, frequently produced free rent for the primary family and help from relatives outside of the household was more substantial.

In summary, the work primary type of income package was comprised mainly of work by the woman and, when present, by the husband. This was supplemented by AFDC and food stamps but always in relation to work and marital status and always as a smaller proportion of total income than income from work. Additional sources were children's earnings and help from relatives both inside and outside the household.

An example of the work primary type is Mrs. D., who is a black woman, aged 39 in 1968, with a high school education. Mrs. D. gave her marital status as "divorced" throughout the ten years (the marriage having ended in 1967) and had two children with whom she lived in a nuclear family unit. The older child moved out in 1971 and then returned some years later.

Mrs. D. worked every one of the ten years, first in clerical/sales, then in professional/technical occupations, and finally as a teacher's aide. The first year after the marital separation she earned $500 working part-time, part-year, the second she earned $1,000 working half-time the full-year, and after that she worked full-time, full-year increasing her annual labor income to $9,000 in 1975. Her hourly wage rose accordingly from $.60 to $6.10 in the ten-year period.

The family received AFDC in 1967 in the amount of $1,500, which decreased each year as earnings increased until in 1970 AFDC income was only $600. After a two-year hiatus, AFDC was resumed for two years yielding $400 each year. Food stamps accompanied the AFDC grant in small amounts in 1973, 1974, and 1975. AFDC was apparently taken up again after two years because children's earnings had ceased for that time. There may also have been a welfare policy change that upgraded the stipend and again made Mrs. D. eligible for a small supplement. The only other sources of income acknowledged were children's earnings, which were reported for six of the ten years and in the highest year amounted to $5,000.

Although this case is somewhat atypical in its lack of complexity, it illustrates graphically the close relationship between work and welfare that is characteristic of the work primary type. Mrs. D. increased her work effort and her earnings from the time that her marriage ended and used AFDC and food stamps decreasingly as a supplement to work. The AFDC income was also affected by children's earnings, which were important in this income package.

In summary, these three types of center-city, welfare-risk families had much in common but also had rather different kinds of income packages that were in turn accompanied by different sorts of family and household structures. The woman's attachment to work may have been nonexistent, supplementary, or primary. Concomitantly, occupations ranged from domestic work only in the welfare career group to mainly domestic work in the welfare primary type to higher level jobs in the work primary group. Hourly wages also increased accordingly. The use of AFDC and food stamps was continuous and intensive in the first group, intermittent but still primary in the second, and supplementary in the last. While all types made use of children's earnings, child support, relatives' help and boyfriends' contributions they did so differentially. Family and household structure also varied with this typology, ranging from many marital or quasi-marital liaisons and residential units that consisted of related and unrelated others in the welfare career group to fewer such unions and more nuclear family units among the work primary types.

TRANSITION POINTS IN WORK AND WELFARE DECISIONS

The methodology that is used here—qualitative analysis of quantitative data—lends itself most profitably to observing the context from which work and welfare decisions emerge. Here the variety of factors that impinge upon such transition points can be isolated and understood as they interact to produce such decisions. We have therefore noted these passages from one status to another to determine the events that affect and surround them.

Work often started when older children who had earnings moved out, or was resumed after the birth of a child when the child reached one or two years of age. Labor income frequently stopped when a woman separated from her husband, at which time AFDC was taken up. Another pattern was for work to be reduced or to stop when the woman remarried. In one instance, work ceased because of a severe disability.

The receipt of AFDC income typically started when the woman's labor income was decreased or became nonexistent, or when she became separated. It also commenced when children were born (because work stopped) or when grandchildren moved in, making the woman an "eligible payee" for welfare purposes. AFDC income was also initiated when other sources of income such as children's earnings or child support disappeared or were diminished. AFDC income typically stopped when a woman remarried or when her labor income reached the cut-off point. Less often, it ceased when other income sources became substantial enough to end AFDC eligibility. In one instance, the receipt of social security benefits put an end to income from AFDC.

The primary link then was between work and welfare although marital status was also very decisive. Other sources of income played a less significant role in producing changes in work and welfare statuses but were most influential when combined with work, welfare, and marital factors. The complex nature of events that surrounded such transition points can best be illustrated by some case examples.

Mrs. E. (always-female-headed) worked for five years earning a substantial salary. In 1972 she stopped working and began to receive AFDC and food stamps, which continued throughout the remaining five years. However, after one year of not working, she resumed work for the remainder of the ten-year period although she drastically reduced her work effort, with AFDC being the primary source of income. The changes from work only to AFDC only to welfare primary were brought about by two events. Her older children, who had previously had rather high earnings, moved out and a second grandchild moved in. Mrs. E. now became more eligible on two counts—her children's earnings were no longer available to her, and her two small grandchildren were eminently eligible for AFDC. In addition, the grandchildren probably needed her care at home.

Mrs. F. (always-female-headed) worked every year for six years, earning a variable but adequate salary which was supplemented by small amounts of AFDC and food stamps. She ended her AFDC receipt in 1973 when only one child under 18 remained in the home, and when she acquired access to free rent. Her labor income was now too high to permit AFDC eligibility since her needs had decreased. She continued to work until three years later when she became severely disabled. At that time, she received social security (disability insurance) and also a large lump sum payment that might have been compensation for her injury. Neither work nor welfare were income sources any longer.

Mrs. G. (changed-status) was married for seven years and depended on her husband's very substantial earnings but worked three of those years supplementing his income. Their children also worked for three years. Mrs. G. then separated from her husband and had a baby, ostensibly from a boyfriend who contributed the first year. The children's earnings also stopped at this time. Mrs. G. then began to receive full AFDC and food stamp grants, having ceased her work effort. The decision to stop work and go on welfare was the result of marital separation, the birth of a new baby, and the cessation of older children's earnings.

From these situations it can be seen that work and welfare decisions are intricately interrelated. While the context of both routes is the need for income maintenance, and this is determined by familial events that produce or obliterate other income sources, the choices to be made between work and welfare (or combinations of both) invariably are affected by the availability of (eligibility for) welfare and the feasibility of work—getting a job that pays a reasonable wage and not having the problem of the care of small children.

THE LEVELS AND STABILITY OF INCOME PACKAGES

In this center-city population the income package is made up of a variety of income sources that change frequently over time. This variety is the response to the inability of any one sourcce to effect an adequate total income, while fluidity is brought about by changing life circumstances, labor market opportunities, and varying transfer policies. Actual sources depend upon what is available and what is feasible at any one time; within these parameters, rational choices are made as to what would afford a maximum level of well-being.

There are a multitude of factors that determine what composes the income package. As noted before, the opportunity for work and eligibility for AFDC are primary, while marital status follows closely in importance. Other less significant factors include nonmarital unions accompanied by a male's support, children's earnings, the birth of a new baby, relatives' help, the movement in and out of related and unrelated household members, illness, and the availability of transfers other than welfare.

Although the three types of families delineated above had the same diversity of income sources throughout the years, changes in amounts and sources (the fluidity of the income package) varied. In welfare career families, the receipt of AFDC was a more stable factor than in the other types. Conversely, in work primary families, labor income had this kind of continuity. There was more diversification over time in the middle welfare primary group in both work and welfare income. Income from others living in the household, especially unrelated others, was more fluid in type one welfare career cases where such members moved in and out more often. In type two welfare primary families, more frequent marriages or quasi-marriages created instability in the availability of male labor income. Finally, type three, the work primary group, displayed more occupational mobility with labor income usually increasing and producing related changes in the receipt of AFDC and other income sources.

Responses to such continuously changing events may be seen as income coping or income maximizing strategies. It would be of interest, therefore, to note the level of total income that is accrued by such households. In welfare career families, ten-year average annual incomes ranged from $2,710 to $8,961 with a mean total income of $5,304. In welfare primary families, the income spread was from $4,746 to $13,738 with the mean at $7,433; while in work primary families, incomes went from $5,160 to $11,837, the average being $7,375.

As was expected, these incomes are fairly low on average, although not below subsistence standards. It is of interest to observe that the group that derived its basic income from welfare with no or very little work (type one) had a substantially lower mean total income than any other group. Type two, which essentially combined work and welfare with welfare being primary, did the best and even slightly better than type three, those who combine work and welfare with work being primary. This is certainly a testament to the low salaries that these women earn and the corresponding competitiveness of the welfare grant in relation to earnings.

The accuracy of these total income levels is threatened by several factors. Of primary importance is the income of others—anyone living in the household other than head and spouse. In fact, the rather surprising variance in total household income within groups is almost entirely due to the degree to which others' income is present. Whether to include such income is open to controversy. The decisive question is, of course, to what extent these others pool their income with the basic family unit. The PSID counted such income, on the assumption that others share. But in practice, actual sharing may range from contributing nothing to contributing everything. The degree of pooling may also depend upon who the others are and what their sources of income consist of. Children's earnings, for example, would seem more likely to be allotted to the family kitty than the social security pension of an aged parent. We have decided here to include all such income in total household income because it appears to be a fairly significant determinant of work and welfare decisions and it seems reasonable to conclude that, at minimum, rent and utility expenses are shared. Nevertheless, since the magnitude of such sharing is not known, actual disposable income that is available to the family unit may be inflated by the assumed blanket contribution of others.

Another factor that undermines the accuracy of given income levels is the exclusion of the value of food stamps, free rent, and free child care from the "total income" variable.* These, and in-kind transfers from friends and relatives, which may have been underreported or not reported at all, may serve to deflate estimates of actual disposable total income. Finally, there are indications in the data that labor income (especially from domestic work which was so prevalent here) may also have been underreported in order to avoid jeopardizing AFDC eligibility, thus again potentially deflating reported total income levels.

IMPLICATIONS

One important finding of the qualitative analysis concerns the three types of income packages extrapolated from the data. Although this typology deals with the primacy of work and welfare as income sources,

---

*In the following chapter where a quantitative analysis is undertaken, we added the value of food stamps and the value of free rent to arrive at a more accurate estimate of total income.

it is also an indicator of the degree of welfare dependency that families engaged in. As such, the extent to which welfare was depended upon appeared to act as an anchor or pivotal point upon which other lifestyle factors—both economic and social—hinged.

The data show that the importance of welfare in the family income package varied with the amount and type of work that was performed and the hourly wage of the head. The importance of welfare also seems correlated with the receipt of food stamps and the timing and levels of private transfers such as child support and help from friends and relatives. Family and household structure (the number and legality of unions with males, the conditions under which children were born, and who lived in the household) also appears to have varied with the degree of welfare dependency, as did the fluidity/stability of the income package. In short, the balance between work and welfare seems neither frivolous nor accidental but was, in fact, tied to a total way of life.

Another major finding of the qualitative analysis concerns the thesis of income-packaging. Several studies of ghetto communities using the method of participant observation have documented the diversity of the typical income package of families living in center-city areas.[13] According to these studies, such income was comprised of many sources—work, welfare, illegal activities, gifts from kin and friends, household sharing, roomers/boarders, etc. Furthermore, this income package changed frequently over time. Valentine makes the statement that,

> The detailed phenomena of income and occupations are quite complex and frequently obscure. It appears that under fluctuating and marginal economic conditions, the actual sources of general subsistence and occasional surplus become multiple, varied, and rapidly shifting. A great many individuals manage to garner small increments of income from several or numerous different origins.[14]

In our analysis we found a great deal of fluidity in the income package in that income sources changed frequently over time. However, the use of work and welfare remained relatively stable; it was the ancillary sources that changed more often. As noted before, these secondary sources had a differential impact on the use of work and welfare—depending upon which income package type the family was engaged in. Our analysis further shows that while work and welfare were by far the most predominant sources of income, other minor sources such as the earnings of children, child support payments, help from relatives, and contributions of boyfriends, played a decisive part in the level of total income and in many instances, in work and welfare decisions. The less a family was dependent on welfare, the more impor- tant were these ancillary sources of income.

In summary, it is accurate to say that such other income sources were found in the data. It is obvious of course that certain sources such as income from illegal activities could not be captured by survey data methods. Essentially, it was work and welfare that, according to this ac- count, appear to have provided the base of the income package, although other less formal sources were significant in adding to this base.

NOTES

1. U.S. Department of Health, Education and Welfare, SSA, ORS, *Aid to Families With Dependent Children: 1975 Recipient Characteristics* Study, Part 3, "Financial Cir- cumstances," p. 3.

2. Stephen Leeds, *Income Sources of the Welfare-Risk Population*, The City of New York Human Resources Administration, Office of Policy Research, (December 1, 1973); Lee Rainwater and Martin Rein, "Sources of Family Income and the Determinants of Welfare," Working Paper, mimeographed, Joint Center for Urban Studies of MIT and Harvard University (May 1976), p. 45.

3. Lee Rainwater, *Behind Ghetto Walls* (Chicago: Aldine, 1970); Carol B. Stack, *All Our Kin* (New York: Harper and Row, 1974); Ulf Hannerz, *Soulside: Inquiries Into Ghetto Culture and Community* (New York: Columbia University Press, 1969).

4. U.S. Department of Health, Education and Welfare, SSA. ORS, *Aid to Families With Dependent Children: 1975 Recipient Characteristics Study*, Part 1, "Demographic and Program Characteristics," p. 24.

5. Bureau of the Census, *Low Income Areas in Large Cities*, U.S. Census of the Population 1970 (PC92), p. 16.

6. Bradley Buell and Associates, *Community Planning for Human Services* (New York: Columbia University Press, 1952).

7. Steve Erie, Gordon Fisher, and Liz Dayan, U.S. Department of Health and Human Services, "Preliminary Findings of the AFDC Population Study," internal memorandum, December 3, 1980, pp. 13,14.

8. Rainwater and Rein, "Sources of Family Income," p. 4.

9. These states are: California, District of Columbia, Georgia, Illinois, Maryland, Massachusetts, Michigan, Missouri, New Jersey, New York, Ohio, and Pennsylvania (selected by the Welfare Management Institute).

10. These variables are: head's labor income; wife's labor income; food stamps; head and wife's taxable income; AFDC; other welfare; social security; other retirements; unemployment-workmen's compensation; child support; labor part of business income; asset part of business income; labor part of roomer income; asset part of roomer income; trade; rent-dividends-interest; overtime; help from relatives; income from other sources; wife's asset income; wife's transfer income; others' taxable income; others' transfer in- come; number of other income receivers; income-needs ratio; marital status; state; miles to center city; race; head's education; age of head; number in family unit; family unit com- position; number of major adults; number of children; age of youngest child; age of oldest child; who moved in; who moved out; relatives near; mode child care; paid child care; yearly rent payments; disability of head; occupation of head; number of weeks worked:

head; hours per week worked: head; wanted more work; annual hours worked: head; average hourly earnings: head; occupation of wife; number of weeks worked: wife; hours per week worked: wife; annual hours worked: wife; average hourly earnings: wife.

11. Susan Anderson-Khleif, "Ongoing Research Journal," from the Michigan Project, February–March 1976, mimeographed, pp. 8,30,31.

12. Ibid., p. 36.

13. See Note 3.

14. Charles A. Valentine, "Blackston: Progress Report on a Community Study in Urban Afro-America," mimeographed, February 1970, p. 19.

6

Work and Welfare Patterns: Quantitative Analysis

The qualitative analysis in the previous chapter attempted to capture the processes that led to income decisions and the relationship between factors that produced income outcomes. Thus, only a small number of cases were examined in depth, and income acquisition was viewed in relation to non-income variables such as personal, familial, and household characteristics.

In the quantitative analysis in this chapter, a more traditional approach is taken. A larger sample of 206 cases is analyzed purely in relation to income variables: all of the existing income sources, total income, and the income:needs ratio (a measure of family income to family needs as defined by the official poverty standard). A tabular analysis is undertaken to ascertain the dimensions of the income package in this population in the aggregate. As such, the magnitude and frequency of income factors can be determined, a task that the qualitative analysis could not accomplish.

As noted in the previous chapter, the underlying reason for the analysis of income sources is to question the assumptions inherent in the federal government's work policies of the past 15 years that AFDC mothers essentially are a non-working population and that their almost exclusive source of income is welfare. We would then want to examine work activity over time in distinction to administrative statistics which take note of work in one month out of the year. (The PSID data to be used here looks at the yearly unit, although it is not known what part of the year an income source is received). Since it has been documented that welfare mothers tend to work sporadically rather than the entire year, a more accurate picture of the proportion of mothers who engage in work activity can be achieved through the yearly rather than the monthly time period. We would also want to understand the stability and the variability of work, the interchange between work and welfare status, and the place of other income sources in the income package. More specifically, the questions to be asked are: what are the patterns of work and welfare in this group? How do these patterns relate to other income sources, to the levels of total income, and to the level of economic well-being? Work and welfare are examined in total, that is, head's earnings plus wife's earnings plus others' earnings—and AFDC plus other welfare plus food stamps—and are also disaggregated into their components. Trends over time are investigated wherever fruitful, as the data comprise a period of eight years—from 1970 to 1977.[1]

As noted earlier, 206 cases were selected from a subsample of the 5,000 families interviewed since 1968 by the Panel Study on Income Dynamics at the Institute for Social Research, University of Michigan. Our 206 household units* were chosen by the following criteria: they were living 15 miles or less from the center of a city of 50,000 or more in one of 12 urbanized states; they had a female head in at least one of the interview years; they contained a child or children under 18 years of age; and they had received $299 or more of AFDC or other welfare benefits in one or more years.† The selection of a subpopulation that is welfare-risk and that lives in the inner cores of large metropolitan cities has been elucidated in the previous chapter.

As our sample is an inner-city group of family units that had been on welfare and that had been female-headed at some time during the study years, our analysis dichotomizes the total group in two ways: by the years on welfare and the years not on welfare and by whether the family was female-headed throughout the study years or had become male-headed at some point through marriage‡ (this latter segment is called "changed marital status"[2]). It was felt that during the years on welfare, income sources would be quite different than in the years not on welfare. It also seemed apparent that the presence of male heads in the changed-status group would affect income.

The data was further disaggregated and analyzed by race. Race appears important since blacks are highly over-represented on AFDC rolls and because race apparently makes a difference in work activity as

---

*The PSID survey calls these units families, but this is confusing since whoever lives in the household is considered part of the family unit, even unrelated persons. Here, "households" and "families" will be used interchangeably.

†Responses were "weighted" to insure that the findings would be representative of the general population.

‡The changed-status group had interchanged their marital status between married, and single, divorced, or separated. This group then contains both male and female heads in any one year.

well. Perhaps more important, the "welfare problem", especially as it applies to inner-city areas, is often couched in racial terms by some that see it that way.

Unlike the previous chapter, only income variables are considered. These comprise the components of three broad categories: work, public transfers, and private transfers and also include total income and the ratio of money income to needs. All income amounts are annual totals and actually pertain to the previous year's income; they also have been adjusted for inflation by conversion to 1967 dollars.

The analysis of the data has been presented in tabular form dealing with income means and percentages. To give attention to the research questions posed above, four basic tables were devised: 1) income sources with their means and percentages of the groups that receive them for those with such income (eight year averages), 2) income sources as percentages of total income for the entire group (eight year averages), 3) trends in income sources as percentages of total income, and 4) the relationship between earnings and welfare in ratios, over the eight year period. These tables were constructed to take into account the two dichotomies of welfare status and marital status and are also segmented by race.

INCOME SOURCES BY WELFARE STATUS

Years on Welfare

Table 6.1 discloses the mean dollar amounts attached to all of the income sources available to this population for those who received them and the percentages of the families that received them. Looking at the "years on welfare" figures first, we find that in total, the mean amounts received for work are about 1.4 times the mean amounts received from public transfers in these years, and that public transfers, in turn, yield 2.5 times as much mean income as private transfers. The comparatively high dollar values received from public transfers are not surprising since welfare (AFDC and other welfare) comprises by far the largest component of public transfers and "years on welfare" indicates a preponderance of such income. Concomitantly, the percentages of those receiving welfare are two to three times as high as those receiving income from work.

In comparing blacks and whites, we note that blacks have a 36 percent higher total mean labor income than whites (head's earnings are 25 percent higher, wife's earnings 85 percent higher and others'* earnings

---

*Members of the household other than head and wife.

Table 6.1.
Eight-Year Household Income for Those with Such Income by Welfare Status and Race, 1970–77[a]

Income Sources	Years on Welfare[b]						Years Not on Welfare					
	All (N = 128) Mean–	% Receiving	White (N = 55) Mean–	% Receiving	Black (N = 73) Mean–	% Receiving	All (N = 78) Mean–	% Receiving	White (N = 39) Mean–	% Receiving	Black (N = 39) Mean–	% Receiving
WORK	$1,722		$1,246		$1,895		$4,827		$5,578		$3,572	
Head's earnings	2,102	38%	1,750	36%	2,327	40%	6,086	86%	6,845	79%	5,319	92%
Wife's earnings	1,096	02	194	02	1,311	03	3,573	35	3,819	41	3,109	28
Others' earnings	1,969	27	1,793	31	2,047	25	4,821	38	6,069	54	2,379	21
PUBLIC TRANSFERS	1,217		852		1,274		1,077		539		951	
AFDC	2,171	76	1,969	67	2,284	82	–		–		–	
Other welfare[c]	1,740	30	1,644	42	1,835	21	–		–		–	
Food stamps	521	77	541	76	508	77	466	21	307	13	480	28
Social security	1,025	04	829	05	1,124	03	1,828	03	800	03	1,274	03
Other retirement	840	02	329	04	880	01	465	03	114	03	412	03
Unemployment and workmen's comp.	681	05	574	07	614	03	901	09	809	08	880	10
Lump sum payments	1,453	02	26	02	1,521	01	1,794	04	653	05	1,602	03
Others' transfers	1,307	10	903	09	1,428	11	1,006	06	551	05	1,059	08

	Years on Welfare[b]						Years Not on Welfare					
	All (N = 128)		White (N = 55)		Black (N = 73)		All (N = 78)		White (N = 39)		Black (N = 39)	
Income Sources	Mean–$	% Receiving	Mean–$	% Receiving	Mean–$	% Receiving	Mean–$	% Receiving	Mean–$	% Receiving	Mean–$	% Receiving
PRIVATE TRANSFERS	480		485		365		752		457		707	
Child support	711	24	784	33	666	18	1,082	23	1,134	31	725	15
Free rent	554	02	435	04	241	01	786	03	347	03	625	03
Relatives' help	598	09	730	11	333	08	466	06	190	05	504	08
Rents, dividends, and interest	135	*	21	*	135	*	371	06	199	08	520	05
Income from other sources[d]	402	07	455	07	452	07	1,054	08	417	05	1,160	10
TOTAL INCOME[e]	4,424	100	4,290	100	4,514	100	8,794	100	10,762	100	6,849	100
MONEY:NEEDS[f]	1.24		1.21		1.25		2.45		2.81		2.07	

*Less than 01%.

[a]Averages of eight yearly dollar means, percentages, and Ns.

[b]AFDC or other welfare. The average number of years on welfare for all families was five.

[c]Includes General Assistance, Old Age Assistance. Aid to the Blind, and Aid to the Disabled.

[d]Includes mainly cash gifts from friends and other miscellaneous money transfers.

[e]"Total income" here and in subsequent tables includes the value of food stamps and the value of free rent.

[f]Ratio of total household money income to annual family need standard (poverty line that takes into account size of household unit).

Source: Compiled by the author.

113

12 percent higher), and a 33 percent higher mean income for public transfers (14 percent higher in AFDC, 10 percent higher in other welfare, and higher in all the other public transfers except food stamps, which are essentially the same). However, whites have a 25 percent higher mean for all private transfers except "rents, dividends, and interest" and "income from other sources."

Nevertheless, in spite of much higher mean incomes for blacks in the areas of work and public transfers, the proportions of families that received these incomes somewhat offset the amounts of income received. For example, in the work category, 31 percent of whites had "others' earnings" as compared to only 25 percent of blacks. Even within welfare, twice the percentage of whites received "other welfare" than blacks. More whites also were recipients of public transfers other than welfare—or what might broadly be termed "social insurance." ("Others' transfer income," an exception, mainly comprises welfare type benefits and thus is higher for blacks.) And in addition to higher mean incomes in almost all of the private transfers, whites also showed greater percentages having received them, again excepting "income from other sources" (money gifts from friends), the receipt of which is equal among blacks and whites.

Black household units had a slightly higher total income than whites ($4,514 as compared to $4,290) and also a somewhat higher money:needs ratio (1.25 and 1.21 respectively). It is clear then that black families on welfare do somewhat better in total than whites, largely because more of them had head's earnings and had more of these earnings, and more of them received welfare (especially AFDC) and received more in welfare benefits.

Years Not on Welfare

Turning to "years not on welfare," we note quite a different story. Work, in total for those families who do work, yields a mean income that is more than twice as large as the mean from all public transfers. The mean from head's earnings alone ($6,086) is about the same as the mean from all public transfers (mainly social insurance) and almost twice as high as the mean from all private transfers. The percentages having received head's, wife's, and others' earnings are enormously higher than the percentages having received any other source of income. In the years not on welfare, work was heavily preponderant among income sources both in the amounts it yielded and in the proportions of household units that engaged in it.

When the data is disaggregated by race, we find that whites had one and one-half times the mean income from total work as blacks, with the whites head's earnings and wife's earnings ranging from 20 to 25 percent higher and others' earnings as much as 60 percent higher. The percentages of those that work are also higher for whites, except for the important head's earnings, which is 13 percent higher for blacks.

Unlike the area of work, blacks have a 44 percent higher mean for public transfers in total and in every one of the public transfers. Generally, more of them got these transfers, especially food stamps, which over twice as many blacks as whites received. The mean for total private transfers is also higher for blacks (35 percent) and is higher for all the private transfers except child support where the white mean is one and one-half times as high. Percentages of those who received private transfers are mixed but twice as many whites got child support as blacks.

For the years not on welfare, then, whites with such income had a higher labor mean income although more black heads worked. Blacks had a higher yield from public transfers and more of them received them, and also from private transfers, although child support, the most important private transfer for whites, was higher for whites and was received by a larger proportion of whites. Most significantly, white family units while not on welfare had a 36 percent larger total income than black units ($10,762 and $6,849) and a higher money:needs ratio (2.81 and 2.07) undoubtedly due to the higher labor income that they received.

On Welfare and off Welfare

When we compare the years on welfare and years not on welfare for the entire group, we observe large differences in the proportions of each that received income from these sources. In regard to work, fully 86 percent had head's earnings when not on welfare, and 38 percent when on welfare. (More of the black group increased such earnings when not on welfare.) Wife's earnings rose dramatically from 2 percent when on welfare to 35 percent when not on welfare (with the whites showing more of an increase). Others' earnings also went up by 11 percent when off welfare (with blacks rising only 4 percent and whites 23 percent).

The percentage of families that received food stamps was a high 77 percent when on welfare and only 21 percent when not (this percentage dropped more for whites than for blacks—63 to 49 percent respectively). The social insurances were received by similar proportions of families while on or off welfare although their means were slightly higher when off welfare, while the transfer payments of others in the household went down by about a quarter in both means and percentages when off welfare. About the same proportions of families received child support while on and off welfare although the mean amount was higher when not on welfare. One-third more received relatives' help when on welfare (accounted for by whites).

Total income was twice the amount off welfare as on for the entire group, with whites having two and one-half times the income when off, and blacks having only one and one-half times the total income when off welfare. Money:needs ratios followed accordingly. These larger total incomes when not on welfare are accounted for by huge increases in labor income, both in means and the percentages who received it; the receipt of income from other sources increased not at all or very little in both magnitude and frequency. Food stamps dropped radically in the years not on welfare. The larger increase in the whites' total income when not on welfare is due mainly to their larger overall increase in earnings and to an increase in income from child support.

Years on Welfare

In contrast to Table 6.1, which explored income sources for those families with such income, Table 6.2 discloses income sources for the entire group including those that had no such income. We calculated the percentages of each source of total income, denoting the proportion of the components of total income over a period of eight years.

When we look at the entire group during the years on welfare, we note that during those years, work in total was responsible for only one-third of total income and public transfers two-thirds, so that public transfers amounted to twice the percentage of work income. Under these headings, the head's earnings were only half of income from AFDC and similarly, all of the earnings categories (30.3 percent) were half of all of the comprehensive welfare sources—AFDC, other welfare, food stamps, and others' transfers (60.8 percent). Note that the social insurances represented a very small part of public transfers (2.5 percent) with the bulk of such transfers being welfare or welfare-related. Private transfers accounted for only 7 percent of total income with the largest such transfer being child support (4.2 percent).

Turning to a comparison by race for years on welfare, we observe that blacks had a somewhat higher percentage of total income from work (31.8 percent compared with 28.4 percent for whites) and that this was due mainly to almost five points more in head's earnings. Blacks also derived slightly more of their total income from public transfers, largely because their AFDC income was 11.5 percent higher than that of whites. However, the whites' income from social insurance, although low, was twice that of blacks. Private transfers were decidedly different for each race, whites receiving more than twice as much as blacks, mostly accounted for by child support.

Table 6.2.
Eight-Year Composition of Household Income by
Welfare Status and Race, 1970–77[a]

	Years on Welfare[b]			Years Not on Welfare		
	Percent of Total Income			Percent of Total Income		
Income Sources	All (N = 128)	White (N = 55)	Black (N = 73)	All (N = 78)	White (N = 39)	Black (N = 39)
WORK	30.3%	28.4%	31.8%	90.7%	91.4%	89.7%
Head's earnings	18.2	15.5	20.1	59.0	50.3	72.0
Wife's earnings	.6	.2	1.0	12.0	13.4	9.5
Others' earnings	11.5	12.7	10.7	19.7	27.7	8.2
PUBLIC TRANSFERS	63.3	62.0	64.2	4.1	3.1	5.9
AFDC	37.2	30.6	42.1	—	—	—
Other welfare[c]	11.8	16.2	8.5	—	—	—
Food stamps	9.0	9.6	8.5	1.1	.5	2.2
Social security	1.0	1.4	.6	.5	.7	.4
Other retirements	.5	.9	.3	.1	.1	.1
Unemployment and workmen's comp.	.7	1.2	.4	1.0	.8	1.3
Lump sum payments	.3	—	.4	.7	.7	.6
Others' transfers	2.8	2.1	3.4	.7	.3	1.3
PRIVATE TRANSFERS	6.6	9.6	4.1	4.4	4.5	4.4
Child support	4.2	6.1	2.6	3.0	3.4	2.2
Free rent	.6	1.0	.2	.2	.2	.3
Relatives' help	1.1	1.9	.6	.4	.4	.5
Rents, dividends, and interest	—	—	—	.2	.3	.3
Income from other sources[d]	.7	.6	.7	.6	.2	1.1
TOTAL INCOME	(100.2)	(100.)	(100.1)	(99.2)	(99.)	(100.)
	$4,424	4,290	4,514	8,794	10,762	6,849

[a]Averages of eight yearly percentages.

[b]AFDC or Other Welfare.

[c]Includes General Assistance, Old Age Assistance, Aid to the Blind, and Aid to the Disabled.

[d]Includes mainly cash gifts from friends and other miscellaneous money transfers.

Source: Compiled by the author.

To summarize, for all in the years on welfare, work and welfare comprised over 90 percent of total income. Among heads of families (mostly female if on welfare) blacks worked more than whites. Blacks also received more in AFDC income, although whites had twice the social insurance and more than twice the income for child support.

Years Not on Welfare

Let us examine the same group of families in the years when they were not on welfare. We note that a startling change occurred: 91 percent of total income came from work, almost 60 percent of which was due to the head's earnings. The only welfare-type public transfer received was food stamps, which was an astonishingly low one percent of total income. Social insurance was again small at 3 percent. Private transfers were only 4.4 percent, 3 percent of which was due to child support.

Disaggregating the data by race shows that whites had a slightly larger total work component than blacks, but that black head's earnings were as much as 22 percent higher while whites had significantly higher wife's earnings (13.4 to 9.5) and others' earnings (28 to 8). Blacks had twice the public transfers as whites (5.9 to 3.1) mostly due to food stamps which, though low (2.2), was over four times that of whites. Social insurance transfers showed no important difference. Private transfers were the same overall, but whites had one-third more in child support income. In essence, labor income was by far the most preponderant source of income for years not on welfare, with head's earnings substantially larger for blacks, and wife's and others' earnings considerably higher for whites.

On Welfare and off Welfare

The major change in the composition of total income between years on welfare and years off welfare was a 60 percent increase in total work income; this directly replaced the 60 percent of total welfare income (AFDC, other welfare, food stamps, and others' transfer income) that was lost in the years not on welfare. Most of the increase in work income when not on welfare came from the head's earnings (41 percent) and was accounted for mostly by blacks (50 to 35 percent). The wife's earnings rose by 11 percent while not on welfare and was due mostly to whites (13 to 8.5 percent). The earnings of others in the household rose by 8 percent in total and is explained by the rise in such earnings by whites (15 percent); black others' earnings actually decreased when not on welfare by 2.5 percent. The only other notable change between welfare and nonwelfare statuses was in food stamps; income from food stamps decreased by 8 percent when not on welfare for the whole group with a decrease of 9 points for whites and 6 points for blacks.

Years on Welfare

Whereas the previous table denoted the eight-year composition of income, Table 6.3 is concerned with trends in this composition and il-

Table 6.3.
Trends in the Composition of Household Income by Welfare Status and Race, by Percent of Total Income

	Years on Welfare[a]				Years Not on Welfare			
	1970–71[b] (N=108)		1976–77 (N=128)		1970–71 (N=99)		1976–77 (N=78)	
Income Sources	White (N=50)	Black (N=58)	White (N=52)	Black (N=76)	White (N=45)	Black (N=54)	White (N=42)	Black (N=36)
WORK	17.5%	29.4	9.1	30.6	91.7	92.7	88.9	84.2
Head's earnings	11.7	17.6	4.8	20.6	49.8	76.0	61.2	69.4
Wife's earnings	—	.9	—	.3	12.6	13.5	15.1	5.8
Others' earnings	5.8	10.9	4.3	9.7	29.3	3.2	12.6	9.0
WELFARE	63.5	58.9	69.8	59.4	.3	1.0	1.2	5.2
AFDC	32.3	42.1	38.1	44.7	—	—	—	—
Other welfare[c]	21.3	10.3	19.0	5.8	—	—	—	—
Food stamps	9.9	6.5	12.7	8.9	.3	1.0	1.2	5.2
SOCIAL INSURANCE	4.5	1.3	3.6	1.5	2.9	1.9	1.3	2.4
Social security	2.0	.5	3.5	.7	1.3	—	—	1.1
Other retirements	1.5	.6	—	—	—	.8	.1	—
Unemployment and workmens' comp.	1.0	.2	.1	.8	1.6	1.1	1.2	1.3
CHILD SUPPORT	11.0	4.1	5.0	2.9	1.9	1.7	3.7	1.7
OTHER[d]	3.5	6.3	12.5	5.6	3.2	2.7	4.9	6.5
TOTAL	100	100	100	100	100	100	100	100
	($4,601)	($4,516)	($2,999)	($4,117)	($12,047)	($7,073)	($10,137)	($5,896)

[a]Years on AFDC or Other Welfare.

[b]Average of mean yearly income reported in 1971 and 1972.

[c]Includes General Assistance, Old Age Assistance, Aid to the Blind, and Aid to the Disabled.

[d]Includes others' transfer income, rents, dividends and interest, lump sum payments, the value of free rent, relatives' help, and income from other sources.

Source: Compiled by the author.

119

lustrates these by comparisons of the first two years, 1970 and 1971, and the last two years, 1976 and 1977. Again, composition was determined by taking the means of income sources for all in the group, including those without any such income, and converting them to percentages of total income. To simplify the analysis, income sources were grouped somewhat differently than before into work, welfare (now to include food stamps), social insurance, child support, and other (the minor sources that account for a relatively small part of total income).

For the years on welfare, the comparison between the two beginning and the two end years of the eight-year period shows that work income from all members of the household decreased radically from 11.7 to 4.8 percent of total income for whites, but increased slightly for blacks. These changes were due in the main to the head's earnings, which dropped seven points for whites and rose three points for blacks. The earnings of others went down slightly in both groups.

About two-thirds of the decrease in earnings among whites was compensated for by an increase in welfare; AFDC as a proportion of income increased by over 6 percent while food stamps rose by an additional 3 percent. For blacks total welfare also increased but only minimally, while AFDC rose by only 2 percent and food stamps by 2.5 percent.

The social insurances declined one point for whites (although social security almost doubled), and remained about the same for blacks. Child support for whites decreased substantially by six points thus reducing it by about one-half as a percentage of total income. Child support for blacks also decreased but only by 1.2 percent. Other income rose rather surprisingly for whites from 3.5 to 12.5 percent of total income; this is accounted for by increases in others' transfer income, 3.5 percent, and relatives' help, 3 percent (not shown here). For blacks, other income decreased but only slightly.

Among white households, the later years saw a decline in earnings and in child support that was offset by a greater proportion of welfare and other income such as others' transfers and help from relatives. However, since the latter sources yielded less than the former, total income decreased between the years by as much as $1,600 annually (35 percent). For blacks whose labor income increased, there was also a decline in total income but only by $400 annually.

Years Not on Welfare

During the years not on welfare, both white and black total income from work diminished, but this gross proportion needs to be disaggregated. Among whites, the head's earnings actually increased from 50 to 61 percent as did the wife's earnings by three points; the big decline came in the earnings of others in the household (29.3 to 12.6 percent). Overall work income in the black group decreased by as much as 8.5 percent, with all the individual earning categories dropping correspondingly except for others' earnings, which rose. Taking the head's earnings as most important, we note that among whites such earnings grew by over 11 percent while the black head's earnings declined by 6.6 percent.

Welfare in the form of food stamps grew slightly among the whites but substantially for blacks (4.2 percent). Social insurance (due to social security) dropped slightly for whites and rose slightly for blacks while child support went up two points for whites and remained the same for blacks. Other income increased minimally for whites, but 4 percent for blacks, this last being due to increases in others' transfers and lump sum payments (not shown here).

In summary, total earnings dwindled slightly for whites as did social insurance. Child support and other income substituted for these losses, but even the small decrease in labor income created a total income in the later years that was 16 percent lower than in the earlier years. For black households, income from work decreased substantially and was compensated for by increases in food stamps, social security, and other income. It was the decline in work income that undoubtedly caused a 17 percent decline in total income in the later years.

On Welfare and off Welfare

As the data is quite complex, the best way to analyze differences between welfare and nonwelfare status would seem to be by two variables: head's earnings (as a proxy for work) and food stamps (as a proxy for welfare). In regard to the head's earnings, whites decreased such earnings by 7 percent over the years while on welfare and increased them 11 percent when off welfare. Blacks had exactly the reverse history, increasing the earnings of the head while on welfare by 3 percent and decreasing them when off welfare by 6.6 percent. Food stamps, a form of welfare, went up for whites during years on welfare by 3 percent and also went up when off welfare—but by much less (.9 percent). For blacks, food stamp income rose when on welfare by 2.4 percent and also went up when off welfare but by a larger 4.2 percent. Although both whites and blacks increased the use of food stamps during the years on and off welfare, the increase was more for blacks in the years not on welfare.

Table 6.4 discloses the ratio of earnings (head's and wife's) to welfare (AFDC and other welfare) for all of the eight years from 1970 to 1977; by definition, these ratios involve such income sources only for the years on welfare. The means for work and welfare represent the en-

Table 6.4.
Earnings: Welfare Ratios[a] during Years on
Welfare by Years 1970–77, by Race

Years	All		White		Black	
	Ratio	N[b]	Ratio	N	Ratio	N
1970	36.7%[c]	108	33.1%	51	39.7%	57
1971	22.5	107	13.5	48	30.9	59
1972	35.6	135	34.8	64	36.2	71
1973	45.6	132	72.0	58	44.8	73
1974	59.6	142	75.2	61	50.7	81
1975	49.9	141	54.7	53	47.5	88
1976	21.5	131	6.9	53	30.0	78
1977	39.3	125	10.4	51	55.0	75
Average	38.4	128	36.3	55	41.5	73

[a]Head's and wife's earnings: AFDC and other welfare.
[b]Comprises entire group including those with zero income from these sources.
[c]Table reads: in 1970, earnings represented 36.7 percent of welfare income.

Source: Compiled by the author.

tire group thus including those with no such income. The first observation to be made is that these ratios are very high; that is, while these household heads were in receipt of welfare, their work income was considerable in relation to their welfare income. The eight-year average for all is 38.4 percent and it obviously would have been even larger had the incomes of only those with earnings been considered. We note that blacks had a higher such ratio than whites (41.5 to 36.3). This is consistent with the previous tables that indicate higher work incomes for blacks than whites during the years on welfare.

In looking at trends throughout the eight-year period, we see that ratios are relatively high in 1970, drop in 1971, start to climb in 1972, continue upwards in 1973, 1974, and 1975, and then decline in 1976 and (in total) rise in 1977. It seemed feasible that these variations might be tied to the state of the economy as evidenced by the general unemployment rate. This relationship, in the main, appears to hold true.

Year	Unemployment Rate	Earnings: Welfare
1969	3.5	36.7
1970	4.9	22.5
1971	5.9	35.6
1972	5.6	45.6
1973	4.9	59.6

1974	5.6	49.9
1975	8.5	21.5
1976	7.7	39.3

Source: *Economic Report of the President* (Washington, D.C.: Government Printing Office, 1979) p. 214.

Note that except for the differences between 1971 and 1972, the relationship between the unemployment rate and the earnings:welfare ratio is inverse; as the unemployment rate went up, the earnings: welfare ratio went down and vice-versa. The year with the highest unemployment rate (1975) yielded the lowest earnings:welfare ratio. Table 6.4 has shown that this is true for all categories. Unemployment as a factor might also help to explain why during 1972, 1973, and 1974 the ratios were substantially higher for whites than for blacks. If blacks are generally constrained from labor force participation by such factors as lower skills levels and discrimination, then whites would be more prone to be affected by a slack labor market than blacks. It is not equally clear why in 1977 (1976 income), while the entire group's ratio expanded as the unemployment rate declined, the black ratio increased to 55 percent while the white ratio decreased to only 10.4 percent. It is evident that white earnings fluctuate more widely than black earnings from year to year and this again may be explained by their greater sensitivity to overall economic conditions.

Summary

Three analytical categories have been used to assess the frequency and magnitude of the income sources of members of inner-city populations while they are both on and off welfare: the percentage of people in each category who have these income sources, the proportion of total income these sources comprise, and the ratio of work to welfare.

While on welfare, 40 percent of heads had earnings and an additional 27 percent of others in the household (usually older children) also had income from work. This means that as much as 40 to 70 percent of households had at least one earner during the years on welfare. Slightly more black units had head's earnings and slightly more white units had other earners. In addition to AFDC and other welfare, fully three-quarters had food stamps and 10 percent had transfers from others in the household. The social insurances were used minimally while private transfers also did not afford much income. This population was largely dependent upon means-tested programs and to a substantial, though lesser, extent also had income from work.

When not on welfare, this group turned primarily to a huge increase in work effort. The use of public transfers other than welfare—

for example food stamps and transfer income from others—was reduced. There was a slightly more frequent use of the private transfers with an accompanying small increase in the magnitude of such sources as child support; rents, dividends, and interest (mostly rent); and free rent. Although these households were still linked into the friendship-kinship system in the way of small bits of help from these sources, the major replacement for welfare was work.

Turning to the composition of total income, we see that even while on welfare, less than half of total income came from welfare (AFDC and other welfare). Food stamps yielded an additional 9 percent and others' transfers 2 percent; but still only 60 percent of income was attributable to these sources. The balance came essentially from earnings, with only 7 percent from private transfers. Blacks and whites did not differ much in the use of these components of income except that blacks received slightly more income from work and welfare than whites and slightly less from private transfers. When not on welfare, both blacks and whites had income from work, with whites receiving more from work of others and blacks more from the head's earnings. The social insurances and private transfers did not add much to income for either group.

Trends while on welfare indicate that whites worked considerably less as time went on, while blacks worked slightly more. For all, there was a tendency to depend somewhat more on welfare in later years, with whites showing more of this inclination. The social insurances remained essentially the same as a component of total income while child support diminished. As time progressed, whites replaced less work with more welfare; for blacks, this was reversed. When not on welfare, trends in the composition of income show that for all, there was a slight tendency to work less except that the white head's earnings increased over time (this, however, was more than offset by a dramatic decline in the earnings of others). For blacks, others' earnings increased.

The earnings:welfare ratios—the percentage of earnings to welfare—were quite high for the years on welfare and appeared to be strongly influenced by economic conditions, specifically the overall unemployment rate. This was true especially for whites where a small change in the unemployment rate reflected a large change in the ratio. The black's proportion of earnings to welfare was more stable over time. Blacks too had a higher average eight-year ratio than whites.

INCOME SOURCES BY MARITAL STATUS

Female-Headed Throughout

Table 6.5 focuses primarily on the percentages of household units that received various income sources during the eight-year period between 1970 and 1977. Our first concern is the proportion of units that were engaged in work. Among the families that were female-headed throughout the period, only 33 percent had earnings from the head and as many as 37 percent had earnings from others in the household, generally older children. That others' earnings were more prevalent than head's earnings and netted almost as much mean income is quite surprising and attests to the importance of this income source for female heads. Also interesting is the fact that these findings are reversed when race is considered; that is, among blacks the head's earnings were more significant and among whites others' earnings were predominant. The mean income from the head's earnings was also twice as much for blacks as for whites while the others' earnings mean was about the same for both races.

When we come to public transfers, we note that about two-thirds of these female-headed families received AFDC with no appreciable difference between whites and blacks. About a fifth got other forms of welfare with more whites having this source than blacks, and food stamps were obtained by about 70 percent of all families with a slight preponderance for whites. Transfers of others in the household amounted to a sizeable 13 percent while social security was a source for only 5 percent of all but as many as 8 percent of whites. All in all, with the exception of social security for white units, most of these families obtained their income from welfare (AFDC, other welfare, food stamps, and others' transfers) and some from work. Fully two-thirds had such welfare income while only one-third had income from earnings.

Private transfers in two varieties were important: child support that was received by 33 percent of families (as many as 60 percent of white families and only 16 percent of black families) and "income from other sources" (help from friends) mostly received by blacks (11 percent as compared with 4 percent). The fact that as many families had child support as head's earnings (although the latter yielded twice the income) and a substantial amount had friends' contributions indicates that private transfers were quite prevalent.

Total income at $4,393 was low, with the whites slightly less poor than the blacks, while the money:needs well-being ratio followed accordingly. In summary, the bulk of these female-headed families received welfare income, with a third receiving work income, and child support was significant for whites and casual income from friends fairly common for blacks.

Changed Marital Status

Changed-status families differed from female-headed families in that they contained a male head in one or more years. This apparently influenced the frequency with which work income was accrued. About

Table 6.5.
Eight-Year Household Income for Those with Such Income by Marital Status and Race, 1970–77[a]

| | Female-Headed Throughout | | | | | | Changed Marital Status[b] | | | | | |
| | All (N = 36) | | White (N = 25) | | Black (N = 38) | | All (N = 143) | | White (N = 69) | | Black (N = 74) | |
Income Sources	Mean—	% Receiving	Mean—	% Receiving	Mean—	% Receiving	Mean—	% Receiving	Mean—	% Receiving	Mean—	% Receiving
WORK												
Head's earnings	$1,442	33%	$1,076	24	$1,588	40	$3,985	66	$4,527	65	$4,414	68
Wife's earnings	—		—		2,740		3,185	21	3,506	25	2,666	18
Others' earnings	1,987	37	1,926	40	2,025	34	3,856	29	4,598	59	2,263	18
PUBLIC TRANSFERS	1,259		763		1,286		1,226		951		1,193	
AFDC	2,285	67	2,009	68	2,469	66	2,077	38	1,948	29	2,122	47
Other welfare	1,809	19	1,717	24	1,980	16	1,809	17	1,815	25	1,789	11
Food stamps	540	71	541	76	541	68	506	48	553	38	483	57
Social security	1,315	05	973	08	1,209	03	1,452	02	656	03	1,231	01
Other retirements	908	02	—		908	03	594	03	372	06	581	01
Unemployment and workmen's comp.	419	02	—		419	03	950	08	894	10	914	07
Lump sum payments	1,584	02	—		1,584	03	1,198	03	818	04	1,050	03
Others' transfers	1,211	13	862	12	1,179	13	1,223	07	551	06	1,372	08

Income Sources	Female-Headed Throughout						Changed Marital Status[b]					
	All (N = 36)		White (N = 25)		Black (N = 38)		All (N = 143)		White (N = 69)		Black (N = 74)	
	Mean–	% Receiving	Mean–	% Receiving	Mean–	% Receiving	Mean–	% Receiving	Mean–	% Receiving	Mean–	% Receiving
PRIVATE TRANSFERS	624		313		609		585		539		481	
Child support	962	33	1,043	60	883	16	737	20	780	23	706	16
Free rent	513	03	198	04	358	03	755	03	584	03	625	03
Relatives' help	521	03	194	04	528	03	631	10	604	10	389	09
Rents, dividends and interest	499	02	—		499	03	225	04	220	06	170	03
Income from other sources[c]	624	08	128	04	776	11	576	08	507	06	516	09
TOTAL INCOME	4,393	100	4,283	100	4,464	100	6,861	100	7,948	100	5,838	100
MONEY:NEEDS[d]	1.19		1.16		1.21		1.92		2.14		1.71	

[a]Averages of eight yearly dollar means and percentages.
[b]Indicates a change in marital status between married and single, divorced, or separated at least once in the eight years, and the presence of a male head in at least one year.
[c]Includes General Assistance, Old Age Assistance, Aid to the Blind, and Aid to the Disabled.
[d]Includes mainly cash gifts from friends and other miscellaneous money transfers.

Source: Compiled by the author.

two-thirds of these units had head's earnings while a fifth had wife's earnings and about 30 percent had earnings from others in the household. Although head's earnings were received in about the same proportion by whites and blacks, white heads who worked earned 20 percent more than blacks. In the other two work categories more whites had earnings and had more in earnings, especially in regard to others in the household where a huge 60 percent of whites were in receipt of this source with a mean that was twice as high as the black mean. In the area of work, more white families had earners and those that worked earned more.

Public transfers were quite significant for the changed-status groups: about 40 percent received AFDC with many more black families participating than white (47 to 29 percent), 17 percent other welfare, and almost half receiving food stamps with 20 percent more blacks realizing this source. Others' transfers were also considerable at 7 percent, as was unemployment or workmen's compensation at 8 percent. It was the means-tested benefits that were important as well as unemployment compensation, this last especially for whites where more work took place. Private transfers were also notable with child support received by about one-fifth of families (again, higher for whites), relatives' help by 10 percent, and "income from other sources" by 8 percent. Total income was 26 percent higher for whites largely due to higher mean earnings and more earners, as was the money:needs ratio.

In summary, among families in which there had been a change in marital status, two-thirds had head's earnings, 40 percent had income from AFDC, and half had food stamps. Work played the most prominent part in income-procuring, while welfare, if food stamps are included, was also significant. More whites had earnings while blacks depended more on AFDC and food stamps. Private transfers were considerable for both whites and blacks in the way of child support, relatives' help, and friends' contributions.

Female-Headed and Changed-Status

Although both the female-headed and the changed-status groups lived in the same inner-city areas and had the same demographic characteristics, their income sources differed markedly. Changed-status families had twice the proportion of heads who were earners than female-headed families and over twice the mean income from these earnings. Female-headed families had 8 percent more other earners but about half the mean earnings from this source than the other type families. Racial patterns within this dichotomy indicate that in both categories, more black families had heads who were working and more white families had others who had earnings.

Less of the changed-status group participated in almost all of the means-tested public transfers. About 30 percent fewer of these families received AFDC and 6 percent less had transfers from others in the household. While almost three-quarters of the female heads procured food stamps, not quite half of the other group had this income source. Other sizeable public transfers were mixed: more changed-status families had unemployment benefits or workmen's compensation while more female heads had social security income. Private transfers were variegated in that child support, the most important of these, was acquired by more of the female-headed (33 percent) than the changed-status (20 percent) groups, while more of the latter were helped by relatives. Income from other sources (friends' assistance) was received equally by both type units.

The changed-status households did better overall than those that were always female-headed: their total income was about one-third higher, as was their money:needs ratio. This was primarily due to more work income, in turn the result of the fact that there were male heads present who worked more and earned more. The wife's earnings also added to this income source. Among these changed-status families, mean income from the head's earnings was higher for whites so that not only were working male heads present, but many of them were white males who earn more than black males thus bringing work income for the changed-status group even higher. In addition to differences in work income, those family heads who changed their marital status received substantially less welfare income than the female-headed families, thus again increasing total income (as welfare yields less income than work). The female heads, however, were able to increase their total income substantially due to the availability of child support (a full third of them benefited from this source). Perhaps this is not surprising since more male heads were absent than in the other group, and were evidently contributing in their absence. On the other hand, more of the changed-status families secured help from relatives, which is puzzling as one would expect such assistance to be more forthcoming when no male is present.

Female-Headed Throughout

In Table 6.5 we looked at the percentages of families in each group that received certain income sources and the mean incomes derived from these sources. Table 6.6 examines the composition of income, that is, what proportion of total income is due to the various income sources, or what is the magnitude of the components that comprise total income. In addressing ourselves to this question in the female-headed group, we note that one-third of total income came from work, 57 percent from public transfers, and 10 percent from private transfers.

Table 6.6.
Eight-Year Composition of Household Income by Marital Status and
Race, 1970–77[a] (percent of total income)

Income Sources	Female-Headed Throughout			Changed Marital Status[b]		
	All (N = 63)	White (N = 25)	Black (N = 38)	All (N = 143)	White (N = 69)	Black (N = 74)
WORK	32.7	24.9	37.5	72.5	77.2	66.5
Head's earnings	17.4	7.7	23.4	47.6	43.9	52.3
Wife's earnings	–	–	–	8.9	10.3	7.2
Others' earnings	15.3	17.2	14.1	16.0	23.0	7.0
PUBLIC TRANSFERS	57.3	56.7	57.6	23.1	18.0	29.8
AFDC	34.6	31.7	36.5	11.7	7.0	17.7
Other welfare	8.1	9.1	7.4	4.4	5.1	3.6
Food stamps	8.8	9.7	8.2	3.5	2.6	4.7
Social security	1.8	3.2	1.0	.4	.5	.3
Other retirements	.3	–	.4	.3	.4	.1
Unemployment and workmen's comp.	.2	–	.3	1.1	1.2	1.0
Lump sum payments	.4	–	.7	.5	.6	.4
Others' transfers	3.1	3.0	3.1	1.2	.6	2.0
PRIVATE TRANSFERS	9.6	17.3	5.2	4.0	4.2	3.8
Child support	7.7	15.3	3.1	2.1	2.2	2.0
Free rent	.3	.5	.1	.4	.5	.3
Relatives' help	.5	1.0	.3	.8	.9	.7
Rents, dividends, and interest	–	–	.2	.2	.2	.1
Income from other sources[c]	1.1	.5	1.5	.5	.4	.7
TOTAL INCOME	99.6	98.9	100.3	99.6	99.4	100.1
	($4,393)	(4,283)	(4,464)	(6,861)	(7,948)	(5,838)
EARNINGS: WELFARE[d]	40.8	18.8	53.3	351.	449.	279.

[a]Averages of eight yearly percentages.

[b]Indicates a change in marital status between married and single, divorced, or separated at least once in the eight years, and the presence of a male head in at least one year.

[c]Includes mainly cash gifts from friends and other miscellaneous money transfers.

[d]Head's and wife's earnings: AFDC and other welfare; E/W reads: among all female headed throughout, earnings represented 40.8 percent of welfare income.

Source: Compiled by the authors.

Among whites only one-quarter of income was derived from work, 57 percent (as for the entire group) from public transfers, and as much as 17 percent from private transfers. Black female-headed families acquired more from work income (38 percent), the same proportion from public transfers, and much less from private transfers (only 5 percent).

What are the specific income sources that account for the variations in work income and in private transfer income? We observe a tremendous difference in head's earnings: white families had only 8 percent of income from this source while for black families the head's earnings accounted for almost 25 percent of total income. Blacks received 5 percent more in AFDC benefits, and child support yielded as much as 15 percent of the white's total income and only 3 percent of the black's.

Apparently the black female heads worked much more and obtained somewhat more AFDC income; white female heads compensated for these differences to some extent by the receipt of more child support payments. Still, total income is slightly higher for blacks ($4,464 as compared with $4,283) because of the higher yield that work affords. This disparity is reflected in the earnings:welfare ratio, which is only 19 percent for whites and as much as 53 percent for blacks, and highlights the sharp contrast between white and black head's earnings.

Changed Marital Status

Now we question what comprised total income for the group in which the head changed her marital status: what difference did it make when male heads were present during one or more of the eight years from 1970 to 1977? In the entire group of changed-status families, work accounted for almost three-quarters of total income, public transfers for 23 percent, and private transfers for only 4 percent. Among whites, 77 percent of income was due to work, 18 percent to public transfers, and 4 percent to private transfers. Blacks showed a different pattern: here only 67 percent of the total came from work, as much as 30 percent from public transfers, and private transfers were the same as for whites.

In disaggregating by components, we note that although work overall accounted for more of whites' income, the earnings of the heads of black families represented 8 percent more of total income than that of white heads. However, the wife's earnings were higher by 3 percent for whites and most notably, the earnings of others in the household were as much as 23 percent for whites and only 7 percent for blacks. In the area of public transfers, it was AFDC that threw the balance off: this income source represented 11 percent more of total income for blacks than for whites.

Among changed-status households, whites did better in total, having a higher total income and an earnings:welfare ratio 170 percent higher than blacks. This again was due to a greater proportion of income from work, especially others' earnings. The importance of others' earnings for whites was quite dramatic, representing almost a quarter of their total income. Black families did less well, receiving a full 30 percent of their income from AFDC.

Female-Headed and Changed-Status

A comparison of the female-headed and changed-status groups shows again, as in Table 6.5, that work income was over twice as prominent for the changed-status group; it was especially greater in the head's earnings although about the same in the others' earnings category. Public transfers were two and one-half times as important for female-headed families. This was significant in all the means-tested programs but particularly in AFDC, which was three times the proportion of total income for these families as for changed-status units. Private transfers were twice the size for female-headed families, almost totally due to child support, which was five times as profitable for white families as for black. The presence of a male head in these households resulted in more work income which then became the primary income source for the changed-status families. Although female-headed families had one-third of their total income from work, their main source of support was welfare. In both groups, the earnings of others in the household remained an equally significant factor in the composition of total income. Child support was considerable only for white female heads, comprising 15 percent of their total income.

IMPLICATIONS

The Head's Earnings

To summarize the above analysis, we will focus first on the earnings of the family head. This income source is the most important in relation to the three strategies that government employed to promote work, all of which were directed to the head of the AFDC family.

In the years that families were on welfare, we found that an average of 40 percent each year also had earnings from the head. Among those female-headed throughout, one-third had head's earnings. However, studies using the PSID data and aggregating work over several years have shown that many more women work during longer periods. For example, Friedman and Hausman discovered that from 1967 to 1971, 77 percent of those women who were always female heads worked at some time and 66 percent of the female heads who ever received welfare also worked at some point during the five years.[3] Such figures would lead us to believe that most welfare mothers work at some time, given a long enough time span. Analyses of the work patterns of these mothers have indicated a constant but not consistent attachment to work that is necessary but not sufficient to form the mainstay of the family's survival strategy.[4]

This view is further butressed by the fact that work, although undertaken by so many female heads on welfare, yielded little in the way of improving well-being. Only 17 to 18 percent of total income was accounted for by the head's earnings among those on welfare and the always-female-headed. Similarly, among those who worked, the mean yearly earnings were only $2,102 for those on welfare and $2,340 for the always-female-headed.

When the earnings of the head are disaggregated by race, we find that white and black (female) heads who were on welfare had quite different work patterns. Fewer of the white welfare mothers worked and when they worked, they earned less than the blacks. Over the years, this tendency grew: the white woman's earnings decreased as did the percentage of those that worked. Finally, again over time, the earnings: welfare ratios show that the white head's earnings fluctuated much more widely than the black's from year to year.

Black families, on the other hand, had more heads who worked in the years on welfare and also had higher mean earnings than whites. Black always-female-headed families had earnings which were twice as high as that of the whites. Trends in the composition of income show that the black head's earnings (on welfare and female-headed) increased slightly over the years—in distinction to white's. And both the head's earnings and the proportion working remained quite steady for blacks: about 40 percent worked each year except for 1975 (the time of the highest overall unemployment rate) when only 20 percent had head's earnings.

There is some evidence to suggest that these ever-welfare women's work patterns are fairly consistent with women's work in the general population. For example, between 1970 and 1978, the annual earnings of all black women increased from $4,382 to $5,963 while the increase for white women was only one-third that amount.[5] Similarly, an analysis based on U.S. census data of all female heads (not necessarily poor or on welfare) indicates that between 1960 and 1967, the proportion of total income in black households that came from the head's earnings increased from 39.5 percent to 46.6 percent, while the whites' proportion decreased slightly.[6]

These differing work patterns of white and black women on welfare indicate that the blacks had a stronger and more consistent attachment to work than did the whites. Why this is so bears some speculation. Black women have always been the mainstay of black families, the black male for various reasons having defaulted in the breadwinning role. Black women, then, expect to work for survival and for income-maximization, just as men do. White women, on the other hand, have traditionally been infused with the expectation of male support. When this is not forthcoming, the transition to dependency on welfare is more "natural" than to turn to their own work effort.

This evidence regarding the work effort of black women is in direct contrast to the popular conception and the legislators' image of black women on welfare as non-working, income-maximizing, and heavily dependent upon welfare. While it is true that welfare policy cannot distinguish recipients by race, it is also true that given the differing work patterns of both races, any work policy in welfare will have a differential impact on white and black welfare mothers.

Some broader issues arise in regard to the head's earnings. Although 40 percent of these heads work, some would hope that the other 60 percent could also be exhorted to do so. But work requirements to compel more of them to work or to compel those that work to work more may be misplaced. The problem is not that as a group they do not work but that the female head's work affords little in the way of upgrading total income. Our qualitative findings called attention to the prevalence of domestic work in this population. These were "secondary labor market" jobs that afforded little stability and less fringe benefits. The paucity of work-related benefits such as unemployment compensation and social security again attests to the type of work that was undertaken. It is also noteworthy that the mean earnings of these female welfare heads who worked were equivalent to the mean income derived from AFDC. The yields from work were not competitive with the benefits of welfare.

Incentives in the way of exemptions of earned income would appear to hold questionable promise for increasing work effort if work offers such a small advantage in the first place. In regard to services, the qualitative analysis leaves the impression that formal day care was used minimally as a child care service. The qualitative material also clearly suggests that work decisions are heavily influenced by such factors as the presence or absence of children's earnings, the birth of infants who need the mother's care, changes in marital status, eligibility for welfare, and job opportunities. Although welfare policy should have an effect on these complex decisions, it would appear that its greatest potential impact might be in the area of improving the type of jobs that are available to these women. More will be said about this in the concluding chapter.

Others' Earnings

In addition to the head's earnings, there is a second category of work income that deserves mention: the earnings of others in the household. This source figured in the incomes of from 27 to 38 percent of families depending upon welfare and marital status. It also represented up to 28 percent of total income, and can therefore be considered a major income source for this population. Aside from the availability of the magnitude and frequency of others' earnings, this component is difficult to analyze because, unfortunately, the PSID does not tell us who these other income receivers are (except that they are not heads and spouses) and does not indicate to what extent this income is shared with the family or household unit.

The racial breakdown of others' earnings shows that in all categories, both on and off welfare and female-headed or changed-status, white families had more of these earnings and more of them had other earners. (Black families had more in others' transfer income.) Furthermore, this discrepancy was heightened in the transition from welfare to nonwelfare status and in the difference between female-headed and changed marital status. This is also because between welfare and nonwelfare status there was a positive change for whites: they had more others' earnings when not on welfare. The change was negative for blacks: they had less others' earnings when not on welfare. This pattern also holds for the other dichotomy: changed-status whites received more income from others in the household than female heads; and changed-status blacks were in receipt of less such income than female heads.

One plausible interpretation presents itself here. Although others in the household were mainly older children,[7] an unspecified number were either related or unrelated other individuals such as parents of the head, nieces, nephews, cousins, roomers, boarders, boyfriends, or friends. The qualitative analysis in Chapter 5 tells us that the presence of such others was fairly typical in that small sample, especially for female-headed units. It is possible then that among black families, others in the household consisted largely of such individuals while in white units others were mainly older children. It is to be expected that children's earnings would be more stable and not as radically affected by the cessation of welfare status or the entry of a male head into the family unit. Children would be more likely to leave the household for age-related reasons than economic reasons. Also, when welfare income is no longer available, they would tend to work more (as would heads and wives). Conversely, other related and unrelated individuals, as we have seen in the qualitative exposition, frequently moved out when the female head's work or a male's earnings replaced welfare and their presence was no longer necessary for survival. It is suggested, then, that the others' earnings income component was more stable for whites than for blacks for the above reasons, and indeed this is what the data show.*

Whether this speculation is correct or not, the question still remains as to whether such income was pooled. If and where it was not, total income data may be substantially inflated. Anderson-Khleif analyzed the PSID interview schedules of 92 families over a seven-year period and obtained a more accurate picture of what place others' earnings actually had in total family income. She found that although the PSID survey was predicated on the assumption that such earnings were shared,

> a case-by-case content analysis of the seven-year data indicates that this is a very big assumption. If one looks at the data for each family over time, diverse patterns emerge. It is quite clear that in some families this extra income is crucial. . . . It is equally clear that in other cases, not a cent of this money ever goes for the family good.[8]

There is, then, no way to ascertain the actual aggregate importance of this reportedly very substantial income source for this population. Our qualitative analysis does show, however, that children's earnings often affected work and welfare decisions in the small number of families that we studied.

However, regardless of the extent to which the income of others in the household is shared, its policy importance lies in its potential effect on the total income available to those in the assistance unit. That is, what is to be considered income that is "countable" toward determining eligibility and the amount of the AFDC grant? If the income of children or other related or unrelated members of the household is to be counted toward the needs of recipients, this indeed moves assistance policy in the direction of a household rather than a family means test.

In the early years, the AFDC program was heavily geared toward maximizing the concept of the financial responsibility of close relatives for those dependent upon public largesse. Parents, children, grand-

---

*However, note that there was a large decline in white's others' earnings over time, especially for the years not on welfare (see Table 6.3).

parents, and siblings were obligated to support the applicant or recipient before the state would do so. This principle gradually diminished until, in recent times, there was very little such responsibility remaining in the state regulations on AFDC. For example, in Massachusetts, as of October 1981, the following were considered "non-countable income": all the earnings of children under 14, all the earned income of any child under 21 who is attending school and not a full-time employee, and any earnings accrued by a child over 18 living at home who is working and not part of the assistance unit.[9]

However, the Reagan administration's effort to make basic changes in the AFDC program resulted in federal regulations that mandate that states "count" the stepfather's income toward the needs of recipients. This was the first step toward a household definition of need. But now the President's budget for fiscal year 1983 proposes additional such measures which clearly indicate that others' income should be counted. Based on the notion of the economies of scale of shared living expenses in shared households, states would be required to pay less than full benefits whenever an AFDC recipient lives in a household with others. In such situations, benefits would be prorated and reduced. States would also be required to count the income of all adults living in the household who are not related to the AFDC children as income to the children.[10]

Whether this proposal becomes law or not, the extent to which the state, the family, and household members are responsible for the support of assistance recipients remains an issue of ethics and policy in AFDC.

Welfare

The other major dimension of income that we are concerned with is welfare. Broadly speaking, this center-city population appears to follow the pattern of welfare acquisition that is inherent in its overall counterpart. In looking at 745 ever-welfare families from 1967 to 1973, Rein and Rainwater observed that 20.2 percent of their total income was derived from welfare (AFDC and other welfare).[11] In our group, 22.9 percent of total income came from this source, averaged over the eight year period. The total seven-year income for the Rein and Rainwater group was $40,850 and for our group the total eight-year income was $46,663 thus making them almost identical.[12] In these respects, at least, the subpopulation at issue here does not behave differently. In this sample, as noted in Table 6.1, the average number of years that families were on welfare was five (out of the eight study years).

When welfare receipt is examined by race, it is seen that in all three categories—always-female-headed, changed marital status, and years on welfare—the composition of income was such that black families had slightly more AFDC and other welfare income than white families, except in the changed-status group where welfare was a sizeably larger component for blacks than for whites. Black families, then, were more dependent on welfare than white families especially when males entered such units. Since the black male's earnings are lower than the white's and his labor force participation has decreased over time,[13] a larger proportion of income was due to welfare.

Trends in the composition of income indicate a decline in total income between the first two and the last two years of the study period (Table 6.3). An examination of the reasons for these decreases in all categories—whites and blacks on welfare and off welfare—illustrates the place and meaning of welfare as an income source. Among white families in the years on welfare, total annual income decreased by 35 percent. Although Table 6.3 indicates that welfare became a larger proportion of total income as the years progressed, it actually amounted to fewer dollars. In 1970–71, income from AFDC and other welfare was $2,470 while in 1976–77, it was only $1,713. Only five percent fewer of the whites received welfare in the latter years; it was the mean income that welfare yielded that had declined. Welfare, however, was responsible for only 52 percent of the decrease in total income while work income mostly from the head's earnings accounted for an additional 33 percent. Similarly, among black families on welfare who experienced a much smaller nine percent decline in total income, three-quarters was due to a decrease in welfare income. So for both groups, while dependency on welfare increased, the yields of welfare as an income source decreased over time. In the years not on welfare, white families had a decline in total income of 16 percent which is accounted for by a drop in the earnings of others in the household; black families' total income decline of 17 percent was due to a decrease in the work income of both the head and the wife.

For families on welfare, a loss of some welfare income was the principal reason for a decline in total income—and therefore, in well-being. Kasten and Todd, looking at AFDC families in the PSID data, found that "the average ratio of income to the poverty line for families receiving most of their income from AFDC fell by 24 percent between 1969 and 1977." They explain this by the fact that the average AFDC benefit declined by 19 percent (in constant dollars) between 1969 and 1979.[14] The increase in food stamp income after the 1974 consolidation and federalization of the food stamp program was experienced by our sample and somewhat mitigated the devaluation of the AFDC benefit, but not enough to prevent a decline in total income.

To get some notion about the magnitude of this decline, the total income of white and black families during the years on welfare was compared with the U.S. median income in constant dollars for all families. In our sample, for white families in 1969–70, total income represented 52 percent of the U.S. median for white families. In 1975–76, however, it was only 33 percent. The relative decline for black families was not as sharp. In the early years, our black families' total income was 83 percent of the U.S. median for black families; by the later years it had decreased to 76 percent of the median. In both groups there was a relative as well as an absolute reduction. The U.S. median for all families on the other hand, remained almost identical in the early and later years for both whites and blacks.

The obvious question here that concerns policy is: At what level of well-being should society choose to support welfare recipients? The fact that there has been a decline in this level should bring this issue to the forefront. A major obstacle to raising the welfare benefit lies in its potential to act as a work disincentive. It is also to be remembered, however, that incentives and disincentives are most effective when choice is expanded, and have the least impact when choice is constricted. In these years of high unemployment rates, the disincentive possibilities of higher welfare benefits should be less of a factor, if a factor at all in such a decision.

Income-Packaging

The theory of income-packaging indicates a "piecing together" strategy from various bits and sources in order to maximize total income. Several qualitative studies have called attention to the kind of income-packaging that poor, inner-city families engage in. Total income is said to be comprised of a variety of sources: work, welfare, children's earnings, child support, boyfriends' contributions, rent, illegal activities, and gifts and loans from kin and friends. Here, while the first four sources did add greatly to income, the informal private transfers such as rent, relatives' help, and "income from other sources" (under which many of these sources would be coded) did not appear to be numerically important. Neither did such formal sources as the work-related benefits (social security, unemployment compensation, etc.) contribute more than minimally to total income. Only the work of various family members, the means-tested benefits (AFDC, other welfare, food stamps, and others' transfers), the private transfer, and child support were important in these income packages.

In fact, these inner-city total incomes showed less diversity overall than those of other ever-welfare families. In the Rainwater and Rein account, work-related benefits comprised four percent of income for those on welfare and 12 percent for those not on welfare. Our data (Table 6.2) shows infinitely smaller percentages. Similarly, private transfers in their report were 13 percent for families on welfare and 19 percent for those not.[15] Our figures are seven and four percent respectively.

Our sample had little work-related benefit income and not much in the way of private transfers (except for child support). It can be assumed that work-related benefits were not prevalent because of the nature of the work that was undertaken and the tenuous attachment to the primary labor market. Private transfers in the Rainwater and Rein account include only alimony, child support, and help from relatives. Our group apparently had less access to these sources, too. A more pressing issue, however, is the absence of informal income such as gifts, loans, illegal income, and cash or in-kind exchanges that the qualitative studies show.

Several possibilities present themselves. One might argue that the magnitude of such informal sources cannot be captured by survey research since respondents would have much to lose by disclosing their true dimensions. Qualitative methods that involve participant observation and other such intensive field techniques would be more likely to ascertain accurately how significant this kind of income is for the total income package. (By the same token, such studies would also have greater access to actual rather than reported earnings.) Another thought is that certain such income may not be measurable, for example, loans that are defaulted on, exchanges of goods, and so on. Other income sources such as those derived from illegal activities are not reportable; short-run, crisis income may not be reportable. To capture many of these sources, monthly rather than yearly surveys would be more effective. Finally, the magnitude of all these informal income sources may be overestimated by qualitative studies and thus not show up here.

There are important policy issues attached to these informal sources of income for welfare recipients regardless of the fact that the extent to which they exist is really unknown. Assuming that there is such diversity in the income packages of many welfare families, especially those that live in the center-cities of large metropolitan areas, the question that arises is whether government should support and encourage such diversity. If there are fewer components in the package, it is easier for welfare officials to be aware of and control them. In addition, less components and therefore less total income will tend to create less disincentives to work effort. On the other hand, the more diversity, the larger the income and the more adequate the level of living that it affords.

Another issue is whether such informal income should be *counted* as income that would reduce the welfare grant or obliterate eligibility altogether. As we have seen, in real terms, benefits have already been reduced quite substantially over the years, as, consequently, has total income. Would it therefore be sound policy to further lower the welfare grant? Conversely, if such informal income is not counted, the state may be duplicating recipients' income, thus opening up the possibility of servicing people who are not really in need. Although state need standards are relatively low, they are based on the premise that recipients have only reported sources of income.

Finally, the question has been raised by proponents of self rather than government help, as to whether governmental intervention destroys such informal sources of assistance. Nathan Glazer alleges that:

> every piece of social policy substitutes for some traditional arrangement, whether good or bad, a new arrangement in which public authorities take over, at least in part, the role of the family, of the ethnic and neighborhood group, or of the voluntary association. In doing so, social policy weakens the position of these traditional agents, and further encourages needy people to depend on the government rather than on the traditional structures for help.[16]

The same issue can, however, be interpreted differently. If informal sources supplement rather than substitute for the welfare grant, it is possible that government largesse acts not to discourage informal sources of assistance but to encourage them. In this view, welfare is the survival base or income floor upon which people build various strategic mechanisms to increase their income and improve their well-being.

NOTES

1. Eight years of data were used in the quantitative analysis of the PSID data rather than ten years as in the previous qualitative analysis because AFDC and "other welfare" were confused by both interviewers and respondents in the first two years.

2. The changed marital status group consists of women who moved from married status to single, divorced, or separated status and vice versa. Consequently, each year there are varying numbers of female and male heads in this group. If we had selected a group composed only of married women, AFDC income would not have been adequately captured. Widows were not included as it was felt that their income sources and work and welfare patterns would be radically different. Also, there are very few widows among the AFDC recipient population.

3. Barry L. Friedman and Leonard J. Hausman, *Work and Welfare Patterns in Low Income Families*, Waltham: Brandeis University, June 1975, p. 101.

4. Mildred Rein and Barbara Wishnov, "Patterns of Work and Welfare in AFDC," *Welfare In Review* 9, no. 6 (November–December 1971).

5. Steven H. Sandell, "Family Income in the '70s: the Demographics of Black-White Differences," mimeographed, October 1980, p. 13.

6. Suzanne M. Bianchi, "Racial Differences in Per Capita Income, 1960–76: The Importance of Household Size, Headship, and Labor Force Participation," *Demography* 17, no. 2 (May 1980): p. 132.

7. Susan Anderson-Khleif, "Income Packaging and Life Style in Welfare Families," Family Policy Note 7, Joint Center for Urban Studies of the Massachusetts Institute of Technology and Harvard University, Winter 1978, mimeographed, p. 10.

8. Anderson-Khleif, "Income Packaging and Life Style," p. 12.

9. The Commonwealth of Massachusetts, Department of Public Welfare, *State Letter 553*, September 29, 1981, mimeographed, pp. 1,2.

10. U.S. Office of Management and Budget, *Major Themes and Additional Budget Details, FY 1983*, p. 51.

11. Martin Rein and Lee Rainwater, "Patterns of Welfare Use," *Social Service Review* 52, no. 4 (December 1978): p. 522.

12. Rein and Rainwater, "Patterns of Welfare Use," p. 522.

13. Sandell, "Family Income in the '70s," pp. 13, 15.

14. Richard A. Kasten and John E. Todd, "Transfer Recipients and the Poor During the 1970s," paper prepared for the Second Research Conference of the Association of Public Policy Analysis and Management, October 24 and 25, 1980, pp. 8, 11.

15. Lee Rainwater and Martin Rein, "Sources of Family Income and the Determinants of Welfare," Joint Center for Urban Studies of the Massachusetts Institute of Technology and Harvard University, May 1976, mimeographed, p. 53.

16. Nathan Glazer, "The Limits of Social Policy," *A Commentary Report* 1971, (New York: Commentary Magazine, 1971) p. 4.

7
Conclusions

Since 1967 the major emphasis in welfare policy has been on work for welfare recipients as a means to reducing AFDC costs and caseloads, comprised mainly of welfare mothers. To effect this goal, the 1967 amendments to Title IV-A of the Social Security Act created the WIN Program, which made mandatory the registration of every "appropriate" AFDC recipient for work and training, placed a new emphasis on social services largely geared to reducing dependency, and instituted the thirty and one-third work incentive. Neither the WIN work requirement nor the thirty and one-third work incentive appeared to have any effect on the work behavior of AFDC mothers. Social services, too, have had the same negligible impact on this goal. The rate at which AFDC mothers are reported to work while they are on welfare has remained at a constant 14 to 16 percent of the caseload;[1] case closings for employment-related reasons also have been stable at about 7 percent.[2] By the early 1970s, work for female heads of families became increasingly acceptable as more and more nonwelfare female heads entered the labor force. Paradoxically, at this time hope for work as a strategy for cost and caseload reduction was all but abandoned and aspects of administrative reform such as error control became the focus of government action. In effect, government has engaged in the rhetoric but not the reality of a consistent, coherent, and committed policy to promote work. We will briefly recapitulate the findings on the three work strategies as outlined in detail in Chapters 2, 3, and 4.

This chapter is a revised version of "Work in Welfare: Past Failures and Future Strategies," which appeared in *Social Service Review* 56, no. 2 (June 1982).

WORK REQUIREMENTS

The failure of the WIN program to service a significant portion of the caseload and to result in an adequate number of job placements has been well documented. These outcomes can be best understood within the context of WIN's selection practices, program components, and enforcement procedures. WIN's ambitious attempt to include and service a huge number of recipients was thwarted by inadequate funding levels. Since 1975, only $365 million per year has been allocated to WIN—$165 per registrant—a sum that affords only 40 percent of registrants any service at all.[3] To ease this problem, a large proportion of the caseload was exempted from the requirement to register and many of those in the system were left in "holding" or "unassigned" nonproductive statuses. Programmatically, WIN has always been heavily involved in ancillary activities and less directly in work. Initially such program components as orientation, counselling, and basic education consumed a large proportion of limited resources. Although several mandated program changes later moved WIN from education and institutional training to on-the-job training and then to job search, provision of jobs has been a minor effort. By 1980, although the institutional training component had decreased to the point of absorbing only 7 percent of funds, supportive services still commanded one-third of the budget while "intensive employment services" and job placement accounted for only 18 percent.[4] Finally, WIN is less a work requirement than a registration requirement. Participation, especially for women, has been voluntary with very few sanctions applied to either men or women.

The history of WIN sanctions illustrates both congressional and bureaucratic ambivalence about enforcing WIN as a work requirement. Before 1978, sanctions for noncompliance consisted of a three-month period where the noncooperating client was deleted from the AFDC budget. A second refusal netted an additional six-month grant reduction while all other members of the family continued to receive their regular grant allowances. In fiscal year 1978, there had been 49,824 "Notices of Intended Deregistration"[5] nationally but only 24,114 of these actually resulted in sanctions.[6] This oversight of half of the persons who were targeted to be sanctioned documents the reluctance of welfare agencies to pursue this route. In 1978, a court order removed fixed sanctioning periods and mandated the grant reduction only if and for so long as an individual refused to cooperate, with a maximum penalty of 42 days.[7] Fiscal year 1980 saw only 28,702 "Notices to Deregister"[8] of which 14,401 became sanctions.[9] This drastic reduction in intentions to sanction, as compared with the 1978 figures, is attributable to the new regulations that so reduced the penalty period as to make the sanctioning procedure futile. On June 9, 1980, via Public Law 96-25, Congress amended the WIN legislation returning again to fixed sanctioning periods.[10]

Selection processes that drastically diminished the proportion of the caseload that could benefit from WIN, program activities that were not job-focused, and minimal enforcement procedures had the effect of mitigating the intended purposes of the WIN program. It is not surprising therefore that the program had no apparent impact on the work behavior of AFDC mothers.

SOCIAL SERVICES

Social services as a strategy to promote work was first evident in the 1967 amendments. Unlike the services legislated by the 1962 amendments, which had a rehabilitative focus, in 1967 services under Title IV-A (AFDC) were to be concrete and directly tied to work. Self-support for AFDC recipients was explicitly enunciated as a primary goal for social services. The new law also contained two stipulations that later had significant consequences for this goal: an inclusion of former and potential recipients into the group of service eligibles, and permission for state welfare departments to purchase services from private and other public agencies.

Despite the clear emphasis on work for AFDC recipients in the amendments, practice after 1967 was not significantly oriented in this direction. Within AFDC, only a small proportion of services were work-related and those, to a great extent, went to nonworking recipients. A substantial amount of funds was diverted from AFDC recipients to the "former and potential" category and supported services that had no bearing on work.[11] Resistance to implementing the intent of Congress reflected the ambivalence of both the federal and state welfare agencies toward the dictum requiring work for AFDC mothers. At the same time, encouraged by the opportunity of open-ended federal funding, states substituted federal dollars for state dollars and greatly expanded their social service expenditures. Provider pressure additionally resulted in enormous increases in some services via the mechanism of purchase.[12]

As a result, in 1972 Congress put a $2.5 billion yearly limit on the federal contribution and also ruled that 90 percent of service funds were to be used for welfare recipients. In interpreting this legislation, a now conservative HEW attempted to reinstate the focus on work for AFDC recipients through various efforts at producing regulations. However, the continuing and powerful protests of several interest groups such as providers, social agencies, and state legislators prevented such regulations from becoming a reality. The conflict was finally resolved by the passage of the 1974 amendments, which replaced Title IV services by a new Title XX, almost totally reversing the work-welfare initiative of the 1967 amendments.[13]

Title XX retained the self-support goal but added a "preserving, rehabilitating and uniting families" goal that took precedence. It extended services to the middle class by eliminating welfare status as a determinant of eligibility and tying it instead to the state's median income, and made some services available to all without regard to income. It created exacting day care standards so that custodial child care on a scale large enough to service working mothers was no longer feasible. Only 50 percent as compared with the earlier 90 percent of service funds in each state were mandated for welfare recipients through AFDC, SSI, and Medicaid.[14]

Title XX effectively squeezed the welfare and near-welfare poor out of the services arena and took the focus of services off of work. Although still touted as an aid to work for welfare mothers, ensuing practice has belied this myth. Predictably, each year the nonwelfare segment of services recipients has increased and has coopted more and more limited service funds. In 1976, the first year of Title XX's operation, 40 percent of funds was spent on AFDC recipients; by 1980, only 25 percent was alloted to them. Similarly in 1976, 31 percent of service recipients were also in receipt of AFDC while in 1980 only 18 percent were in this category.[15] The extent to which services were work-related under Title XX is also significant. Employment, education, and training services in fiscal year 1978 accounted for only 9 percent of all service expenditures with only 2 percent going to AFDC recipients.[16] Day care for children that was "AFDC training and job-related" represented only one-third of all day care costs, while day care for "income-eligibles" took up over 50 percent of these costs.[17] It can be seen therefore that Title XX focused neither on serving AFDC clients nor on services related to work. The intent that social services become a strategy for enabling work in AFDC has been subverted by the ambivalence of the welfare bureaucracies and the strong opposing interests of other groups. As a result, this mechanism never became a reality and had no impact on the work activity of AFDC mothers.

WORK INCENTIVES

The thirty and one-third exemption of earned income stemmed from the belief that recipients would choose to work if they were permitted to keep part of their earnings. The decreased tax rate on earnings did not however have the intended impact on the work effort of AFDC mothers. Work incentives in AFDC are substantial; they include work expenses, child care expenses, and the thirty and one-third exemption, all of which are disregarded in computing the AFDC grant. In recent years however, many new entitlement programs have come into effect. Benefits from Medicaid and food stamps are also reduced as a result of work, and so the total cumulative tax rate makes work a costly alternative to welfare.

Work effort is sensitive not only to incentives but also to benefit levels. While higher incentives should produce more work, lower benefit levels may have the same effect. Although AFDC benefits have been eroded by inflation, they have in current dollars continued to rise. In 1967 the average monthly payment for a family of four was $162; by 1977 it was $284.[18] Furthermore, the total benefit package has been upgraded by the addition of Medicaid and food stamps. Medicaid alone provides the equal of $165 per month to a four person family in high benefit states such as Massachusetts.[19] When this package is pitted against the typical wages that AFDC mothers can earn in their current secondary labor market type jobs, the rewards of welfare tend to outweigh those of work.

As noted in Chapter 3, the simultaneous reduction in incentives and increase in benefits in the southern states resulted in a 40 to 60 percent decline in work effort between 1967 and 1977. Since the national proportion of working AFDC mothers remained the same during this period, the thirty and one-third earnings exemption did have a small positive effect in the remaining states. However, as a national policy to promote work, it must be judged as ineffective.

In spite of the evident failure of WIN, social services, and work incentives to promote work, the alleged policy commitment to work has not disappeared. Some states have requested and received waivers of federal restrictions to conduct demonstration projects in work for AFDC recipients; others such as Massachusetts have recently set up special "work and welfare" departments to institute work. In light of this persistent interest in work, it should be fruitful to look at both the work experience and the actual work potential of AFDC women.

WORK EXPERIENCE

Although only a small proportion of AFDC mothers work while on welfare, such statistics are deceptive since they capture work at only one point in time. A closer look at their work experience reveals a different picture. Among AFDC female heads in 1977, only 25 percent were never employed.[20] Census and other surveys show that from 30 to 50 percent work at some time during the year.[21] To supplement such data, Rainwater and Rein took a sample of women ever on welfare in a five year period from the PSID and analyzed their work behavior. From 44 to 62 percent had income from their own earnings in each of the five years.[22]

In Chapter 6, we analyzed the center-city group of welfare-risk families from the same survey and found similar work patterns, as we followed women and their families for an eight-year period. The data was stratified into two dichotomies: years on welfare and years off welfare; and female-headed throughout and changed marital status. During the years on welfare, 38 percent of these families had income from the head's earnings and such income comprised 18 percent of total household income. While not on welfare, fully 86 percent of families had heads with earnings that accounted for 60 percent of total income (it is to be recalled that these were families that had had at least one year of welfare income during the eight years). While female-headed, one-third of these families had head's earnings that made up 17 percent of their household income; when they changed their marital status to include a male head, two-thirds had earnings from the head that contributed 48 percent to total income.

It is clear then that as a group, AFDC mothers are not strangers to the world of work. Many more work sometime during the year than are at work each month, indicating great turnover between work and non-work status and short periods of work. Although the PSID data do not tell us whether work was performed during the entire year or for only a part of a particular year, several other studies have documented this irregular part-time, part-year work pattern.[23] It is this practice combined with relatively low hourly wages that results in low net annual earnings. Moreover, many of the incomes derived from such sporadic work patterns come from "secondary labor market" jobs that afford neither fringe benefits nor job security.

While the attachment of AFDC mothers to work is continuing, it is not constant. Work may take place in conjunction with welfare or between welfare periods. It is therefore a necessary but not sufficient source of income and additional sources are needed to comprise an adequate total income. Welfare is the major source for these female heads; other public transfers such as unemployment insurance is a less-used provision; and income from private transfers like child support payments, gifts from kin and friends, and rent from boarders are still another source. The income package is unstable as sources and amounts change with changing life circumstances, and each income component produces a relatively low yield. The value of total income is difficult to estimate as many of these components are derived from informal quarters, but this also varies over time.

WORK POTENTIAL

There is clearly a demonstrated propensity for work, but how employable are AFDC mothers? It is always difficult to distinguish those able to work from those unable. We know from many studies, however, that certain personal characteristics generally have a positive effect on work effort. These include possession of a high school education, a work history, a marketable skill, few children, and older children.[24] The AFDC caseload has been typically regarded as a homogeneous group that is essentially unemployable. In fact, it contains several subgroups with varying degrees of work capability.

In 1977 the distribution of these work-related characteristics among all AFDC female heads was as follows: 24 percent of them had either completed high school or attended some college and 75 percent had worked at some time during their lives. Of those who had worked, 32 percent had been in white-collar occupations, 15 percent in skilled or semi-skilled blue-collar jobs, and 32 percent in service industries. Only 10 percent were unskilled laborers and 8 percent were private household workers. Forty-three percent had no child under six years and 17 percent of these had no child under 12. Forty percent had only one child and an additional 17 percent had two children. It is not known what part of the caseload had all or most of these characteristics that contribute to work proclivity, but given these statistics, it would seem likely that a sizeable group of such recipients does exist.

In fact, the incidence of female heads in the AFDC program with these personal attributes has increased. Ten years earlier, in 1967, substantially smaller proportions of the caseload were in these categories, as is shown in Table 7.1. These suggest two alternative explanations. First, more women in the general population are now working, and families have become smaller, and these patterns are reflected in the AFDC caseload. A competing view focuses on the kind of female heads that are now entering the AFDC program. If high participation rates among traditional welfare-risk families have essentially exhausted this population as some studies indicate,[25] then new recipients are being drawn from different strata of the population. Some clues to the strength of this hypothesis can be found in two Massachusetts surveys, one of that state's ongoing AFDC caseload and another of new recipients. Of the new recipients, 46 percent were high school graduates while only 32 percent of the basic caseload had achieved this level of

Table 7.1.
AFDC Mothers with Work-Related Characteristics,
1967 and 1977 (by percentage)

	1967	1977
High school graduation or some college	18	24
Work history	75	75
Occupation		
White-collar	15	32
Blue-collar	11	15
Service industries	28	32
Unskilled laborers	19	10
Private household service	20	8
Number of children		
One child	24	40
Two children	23	27
Ages of children		
No child under 6	39	43
No child under 12	12	17
Proportion Working	14.9	13.8

Source: U.S. Department of Health, Education and Welfare, SRS, NCSS, Findings of the 1967 AFDC Study, Part 1, Tables 40,41,8,55,38. U.S. Department of Health and Human Services, SSA, ORS, 1977 Recipient Characteristics Study, Part 1, Tables 30, 28, 1, 16, 25.

education. The average number of children in the new families was 1.9 and in the ongoing group, 2. The occupational mix of the new recipients with a work history was 30 percent clerical and sales, 30 percent semi-skilled, and 26 percent service work. Of the total caseload, only 27 percent were in clerical and sales, 22 percent were semi-skilled, and as many as 36 percent did service work.[26] The entering cohort of recipients, by these measures, was clearly more employable.

Thus far, we have noted that although Congress had espoused a belief in work for the AFDC mother, the three strategies of work requirements, social services, and work incentives fell short of achieving this goal. Part of this failure was due to the lack of a strong commitment to a work policy. But the idea that work is a solution to growing AFDC costs has persisted and appears recently to have been vigorously revived. In looking at the kind of attachment that AFDC female heads have to the labor force, we observe that although it is tenuous and sporadic, it is nevertheless substantial. In addition, some significant portion of the caseload is endowed with characteristics that indicate employment potential.

Despite the fact that work strategies have not been effective, the question remains as to why more AFDC mothers do not make a positive work decision on their own, given their work experience and potential. A small proportion do work while on welfare and attain a somewhat larger income package than they would if they did not work. Some also work occasionally without reporting it, thus maximizing the welfare grant without penalty. Still others attempt work without welfare supplementation but find it unreliable and insufficient to meet their needs, and so return to welfare. For those who do work full time and all year, and some poor female heads do elect this option, their resulting incomes are usually either less than or equivalent to an income derived completely from welfare. The tradeoff between the benefits of work and the benefits of welfare and the attending complication of the necessity to manage a home and care for children produces a rational decision that precludes work.

WORK STRATEGIES

Given these conditions, future policy in regard to work has limited options. Government can reduce welfare benefits, raise the wages of existing jobs, supply better jobs, require work, or accept the situation and consider welfare a viable alternative to the low-wage job market.

Reducing benefits to all AFDC recipients penalizes those in the system who are not or not easily able to work. The BJIP, President Carter's attempt at reform, and subsequent welfare reform proposals attempted to mitigate this dilemma by dividing the relevant population (male and female heads) into employables and nonemployables and by providing lower guarantees for the former. Such a solution of formally differentiating subgroups and affording some lower benefits than others is not feasible in a program that is comprised mainly of mothers. All AFDC mothers are caretakers of children; it is this status that insures their categorical eligibility, whatever their degree of work capability. It is significant that in the AFDC-UP segment of the program, which contains male-headed families, there is a 100-hour per month limit on work beyond which eligibility does not exist; this restriction acts as a proxy for establishing a lower benefit for families that contain a recipient who has no child care responsibilities and whose employability status is unequivocal.

Raising the level of wages in existing jobs also does not seem to be a realistic alternative. If implemented on a broad scale, the cost of this kind of undertaking would be prohibitive. Costs could be contained if such an effort applied only to AFDC recipients, but problems of equity between them and the working poor would inevitably arise. The possibility also exists that wage subsidization could lead to purposeful wage depression by employers. Despite this, an attempt was made to institute a variant of the wage subsidy with the creation of the WIN/Welfare Tax Credit in 1971, provided to employers who hire WIN registrants. Significantly, in 1977 although 36,000 such slots were authorized, only 5,000 employers claimed the credit.[27] Furthermore, it appeared that the program was not acting as an incentive to hiring welfare recipients but as a subsidy to already existing hires. Speculation on reasons for the low rate of participation proposes that employers are not aware of the program, that WIN registrants work in small, unstable firms that either do not make enough profit to pay taxes or are able to avoid taxes, and that many workers do not work beyond the 30 days necessary to establish eligibility for the tax credit. These problems with the W/WTC program might indeed emerge in a more generalized attempt to institute a wage subsidy.

The option of accepting AFDC as a nonwork-oriented program, or "reforming our expectations" as Bradley Schiller has put it,[28] is not workable in the context of federal program constriction, overall cost cutting, and shrinking resources. Furthermore, while the number of AFDC families actually decreased slightly in the years 1977 to 1979, 1980 saw the beginning of what appears to be yet another upswing.[29] Ways to contain costs and caseloads will inevitably be sought, and work for recipients persists as the primary mechanism in the service of this goal.

The initiative of actual jobs provision for welfare recipients was an essential component of the BJIP and has become more and more focused on the policy horizon in the last few years. Several variants of a jobs approach are reflected in the demonstration projects that some states have recently undertaken. Supported Work Projects, the Work Equity Project, and Jobs Clubs have been addressed to different groups in the welfare population and have used different strategies to promote work. What is common to all of them, however, is an emphasis on jobs. For the most part, it is too early to tell whether these demonstrations can be effective if extended nationwide.

If it is jobs that are on the agenda, given the limitations on resources and the need for concrete results, it is with great selectivity that such a goal should be pursued. It is our tenet that the welfare population can be differentiated according to certain employment-related criteria, and that a proportion of recipients has a considerable amount of employment potential. The size of this relatively employable group may range from a quarter to a third of the AFDC caseload, and may be even larger. For this segment, it may not be necessary to provide costly training and full-time child care services. And since this is a much smaller category, resources that are typically dispersed over the entire caseload as in the WIN Program could be targeted on such a group with the single purpose of jobs provision.

In recent years the WIN program has emphasized intensive job search by participants in the hope that private-sector unsubsidized employment could thus be obtained. The result was the same kind of low-paying, low-level jobs that would have been procured without such programmatic intervention and a concomitant cessation of employment after short periods of time.[30] Even during WIN's early years, despite extensive training and services, those participants who ended their WIN careers with jobs experienced the same constraints.[31] Public service employment, another favored strategy, had similar outcomes.[32] All previous encounters with work and training programs suggest that such jobs both in the public and the private sector are either not taken or are taken and left very quickly.

Unattractive jobs, whether engaged in by welfare recipients on their own or foisted upon them by the welfare bureaucracy, are not competitive with the total welfare benefit package. Training to upgrade the skills of large numbers of recipients that would enable them to obtain better jobs is too costly an enterprise. A better alternative may be to provide better jobs to a smaller, more employable portion of the caseload. These need not be career-ladder jobs with tremendous mobility potential, but they should pay somewhat more than the minimum wage, include fringe benefits such as medical care, and provide a modicum of job stability. The only service that would be essential in addition to jobs provision is after-school child care that might be attached to the public school system. The cost of such an effort for one-quarter to one-third of AFDC mothers could be minimized by the use of existing resources, that is, some priority for recipients in job markets such as city, state, and federal civil service and Title XX contracts. In 1978 only 16 percent of CETA participants were also AFDC recipients.[33] In addition, such a program would make an ideological commitment to the belief that work and welfare are necessarily and formally linked.

Work requirements in principle have been attached in some measure to all work and training programs and to all welfare reform proposals, but they have failed in fact to produce work. For a work requirement to be effective it should contain a reasonable definition of who is required to work, make jobs available, provide whatever service is needed to make work possible, and enforce sanctions for noncompliance while preserving the rights of recipients in relation to these sanctions. As a work requirement, WIN was not able to effect work. It attempted (in principle) to include almost all recipients and had a very broad definition of eventual employability; however, it did not make many jobs available, provided training to only a minority, and failed to enforce its sanctions.[34] On the other hand, in a venture that was focused on a clearly-defined, selected job-ready group, that provided a needed service to all participants and adhered to appropriate sanctions, a work requirement could become viable, meaningful, and equitable, and a logical adjunct to the implementation of the program.

CURRENT DEVELOPMENTS

As part of the Reagan administration's initiative to reduce the federal budget, Congress passed the Omnibus Budget Reconciliation Bill of 1981 (Public Law 97–35) in late July. Effective October 1, 1981, it contains many radical cost-cutting eligibility provisions for the AFDC program. These are expected to save $1 billion in federal funds and a similar amount in state funds each year. As a result, some 500,000 AFDC families, or 11 percent of the caseload, will become ineligible[35] and 300,000 more will have their benefits reduced.[36] Here, we will address only those provisions that are directly related to work for AFDC recipients—the statutes that concern work incentives, work requirements, and jobs provision.

Work incentives must now include a $75 flat monthly rate for general work-related expenses, a child care exemption of up to $160 per month for each child, and a $30 disregard of earned income per month and one-third of the remainder. The thirty and one-third exemption is applicable for only four months while the recipient is on assistance and cannot be repeated until he or she is off assistance for a full 12 months. Furthermore, the work incentives must be applied in the order given above.

Changes in work requirements include permission for states to establish a Community Work Experience Program (CWEP) "to improve the employability of participants through actual work experience and training . . . in projects which serve a useful public purpose."[37] A recipient is required to work in these public service jobs for a specified number of hours to equal his or her AFDC grant divided by the minimum wage. Exemptions from CWEP parallel those in the WIN Program, except that a person already working 80 or more hours a month need not participate, and a recipient with a child under three years of age is excused. (WIN regulations exempt those with children under six.)

Other work requirements permit states to institute WIN demonstration projects in lieu of WIN for a period of three years, if these projects are approved by the secretary of HHS. The states may also change the WIN exemptions to include: only children under age 19 who are attending secondary or vocational schools (previously those attending college were also exempt) and the parent or other caretaker relative of a child under six who is "personally providing care for the child with only very brief and infrequent absences from the child."[38] (Previously this had read simply "the caretaker of a child under 6.") Furthermore, the unemployed parent segment of the AFDC program has been revised from certifying either parent in an intact family as the unemployed parent to eligibility for only the "principal earner," that parent who has earned the most in the preceding 24 months. If that parent refuses employment, aid to the entire family ceases, whereas before only the mother or father was deleted from the AFDC grant.

The jobs provision aspect of the new law permits states to establish Work Supplementation Programs which are, in effect, job subsidization programs to include jobs in government, nonprofit agencies, and proprietary agencies offering day care services. States will decide which groups of recipients are eligible, but accepting jobs will be optional for recipients. AFDC benefit funds matched by the federal government will be the primary source of support for such subsidies, but states will be permitted to supplement such funds with money they save by lowering the standard of need throughout the state, instituting different needs standards in different parts of the state, varying needs standards for different categories of recipients, adjusting benefit levels to take into account benefits from other programs, and reducing or eliminating the earned income exemption.[39]

WORK INCENTIVES

In contrast to some of the work requirement features of the new law that are optional, changes in work incentives are required of state welfare agencies. In essence, the new provisions drastically reduce incentives by raising the tax rate on earnings and lowering benefits correspondingly for working recipients. The $75 flat work-related expense was paid "as incurred" before, with some states setting more liberal maximums, and in fact averaged $95 monthly in 1979. Inflation would have increased this figure by 1981.[40] But even more critical is the order in which the thirty and one-third disregard is to be applied. Up until now, $30 and one third of remaining earnings were exempted first; the new regulation puts one-third of the remainder last, after work expenses and child care expenses, when remaining income is substantially lower. Still more significant is the total elimination of the thirty and one-third after its application for four months, and its unavailability until a full 12 months of nonassistance status has passed. Except for a brief four-month period, the tax rate on earnings will now revert to 100 percent. The problem is further complicated by a related provision of the new law that sets AFDC eligibility at 150 percent of the state's need standard so that many working recipients will exceed this maximum when the disregard ends. A letter from the governor of Massachusetts to the secretary of HHS expresses the fear that "if a recipient anticipates that his income will render him ineligible, he might voluntarily terminate employment or reduce his earnings before the end of the fourth month."[41] It is clear that whatever efficacy work incentives had before will now be largely diminished, and that this is bound to have a negative effect on work effort.

WORK REQUIREMENTS

The major innovation in work requirements is CWEP which, despite the stipulation that the payment of aid is not to be construed "as compensation for work performed",[42] and despite certain safeguards protecting participants, is "workfare" nevertheless. As such, it provides poor work situations and no salaries; and although the program is supposed to prepare recipients for labor market jobs, it is difficult to see how under these conditions it can provide either training or motivation. CWEP does not offer work incentives, nor does it call for strict sanctions with the penalty for noncompliance being the deletion from the budget of only the uncooperating individual as in the WIN program. While CWEP is optional for the states, participation will be mandatory for whichever groups of recipients the states deem eligible. Furthermore, states will now be permitted to induct mothers with children of ages from three to six into the program. Giving the states this kind of leeway without the federal intervention that imposed restraints on WIN participation may create work requirements that are much more restrictive than WIN's.

Another modification in the new law concerns WIN demonstration projects. "A state shall be free to design a program which best addresses its individual needs, makes best use of its available resources, and recognizes its labor market conditions."[43] Other than criteria for participation, which must be uniform throughout the state, "the components of the program may vary by geographic area or by political subdivision."[44] These conditions again give a great deal of leeway to the states in the design of a program and may in fact lead to more stringent practices than are currently in effect in WIN. Massachusetts is a case in point. This state has designed a variant of WIN that is more comprehensive than WIN and also more constrictive. One of its components is

CWEP, which may be mandatory even for mothers with children from three to six years of age. In addition, the entire family will cease to receive AFDC payments if the program participant defaults. The principle of failure to cooperate for "good cause" is also in jeopardy.

> Under the demonstration, the Department of Public Welfare will simplify the adjudication process by limiting "good cause" for refusing to seek, accept and maintain work, by eliminating counseling periods and imposing meaningful sanctions.[45]

These strictures apply to all segments of the demonstration program, not only to the CWEP segment as the law mandates. The plan may not be approved by HHS, but it is interesting to note that a liberal state such as Massachusetts has taken such a hard stance.

Changes in the law also are relevant to the unemployed parent program. In Califano v. Westcott (1979)[46] the Supreme Court ruled that mothers' as well as fathers' unemployment could be considered the basis for eligibility, which meant that the father could be employed and the family could receive benefits on the basis of the mother's unemployment. Contrary to expectations, in December 1980 only 6,000 families or 3 percent of the caseload received AFDC-UP grants because of the unemployment of the mother.[47] Nevertheless, the new law limits such eligibility by selecting only one parent, the principal earner who has earned the most in the preceding 24 months, as eligible. Although the new regulations do not refer to the employment of the other parent, in the spirit of the new law it seems very likely that further regulations or other federal guidelines will establish such employment as a condition of ineligibility. The result will be to limit work effort in intact families to one parent, and so family work effort will be diminished.

JOBS PROVISION

The jobs provision segment of the new law, the Work Supplementation Program (WSP),[48] permits and encourages states to provide a job alternative to the AFDC benefit for recipients who choose such an option. The state welfare agency can subsidize jobs in certain sectors of the economy; it can also decide upon the types of jobs to be subsidized, the wages to be paid, and the duration of such jobs. Thus, there is no safeguard in the federal regulations regarding any of the conditions that adhere to work opportunities. It seems improbable therefore that state agencies will select recipients who are employable and job-ready; provide jobs that pay more than the minimum wage; and provide jobs that afford stability and fringe benefits since no such protective mechanisms are inherent in the federal law.

The other issue in WSP is funding. Basic funding will come from AFDC benefit funds that would have been available had the state not had such a program. But the new regulations give the states permission to obtain additional funding for job subsidization from some rather unlikely sources: states will be permitted to reduce and vary the standard of need by geographic location, by recipient category, and by the availability of other program benefits. They will also be able to reduce the needs standard throughout the state and to reduce or eliminate the thirty and one-third work incentive if they deem this advisable in relation to WSP. In short, states will now be able to pay differential benefits to different groups of recipients or simply reduce the AFDC grant overall at their own discretion and without benefit of a uniform federal policy directive.

Such stipulations have extraordinarily significant effects on the principles and intent of the entire AFDC program that should not go unnoticed. For one, not treating recipients uniformly is discriminatory, against the stated purpose of the Social Security Act, and may in fact be unconstitutional. Second, allowing different payments to different groups of recipients represents an attempt to categorize employables and unemployables without any safeguards attending such decisions. And third, reducing or eliminating the work incentive for those voluntarily choosing employment is in direct opposition to the work incentive principle and will undoubtedly work against increasing work effort.

SUMMARY

It is quite evident that the overall reduction of work incentives will lead to diminished work effort, that the federal work requirements will result in restrictive state practices, and that job subsidization may fall short of providing jobs that afford attractive wages, stability, and fringe benefits. However, since the states have so much leeway under the new law, both in terms of electing programs and in their implementation, future practice will very much depend upon state initiatives. A state could, for example, take the WSP option and implement it in a creative and nonpunitive manner, paying heed to sound participation principles and affording jobs with some promise. States are also not compelled to institute workfare, although they must enforce the reduction of work incentives. The new law has provided many restraints to, and some enablements for, a committed, coherent, and conscientious work policy in AFDC. The route that the states choose will be decisive.

NOTES

1. U.S. Department of Health, Education and Welfare, Social and Rehabilitation Service, National Center for Social Statistics, *Findings of the 1967 AFDC Study*, Part 1, "Demographic and Program Characteristics," (July 1970), Table 38; U.S. Department of Health, Education and Welfare, Social and Rehabilitation Service, National Center for Social Statistics, *Findings of the 1971 AFDC Study*, Part 1, "Demographic and Program Characteristics," (December 1971), Table 21; U.S. Department of Health and Human Services, Social Security Administration, Office of Research and Statistics, *1977 Recipient Characteristics Study: Aid to Families with Dependent Children*, Part 1, "Demographic and Program Characteristics," (June 1980), Table 25.

2. U.S. Department of Health, Education and Welfare, Social and Rehabilitation Service, *Reasons for Discontinuing Money Payments to Public Assistance Cases*, NCSS Report A-11 (July–September 1970), Table 4; U.S. Department of Health, Education and Welfare, Social and Rehabilitation Service, *Reasons for Discontinuing Money Payments to Public Assistance Cases*, NCSS Report A-12 (July–September 1975), Table 6; U.S. Department of Health, Education and Welfare, Social and Rehabilitation Service, *Reasons for Discontinuing Money Payments to Public Assistance Cases*, NCSS Report A-12 (July–September 1978), Table 6.

3. U.S. Department of Health, Education and Welfare, U.S. Department of Labor, National Coordination Committee Work Incentive Program, memorandum from Merwyn S. Hans, November 26, 1980, pp. 13,14.

4. U.S. Department of Health, Education and Welfare, U.S. Department of Labor, National Coordination Committee Work Incentive Program, Letter and Charts: "Grants to States and Program Direction and Evaluation," March 26, 1981.

5. U.S. Department of Labor, Employment and Training Administration, Employment Security Automated Reporting System (ESARS), (unpublished) U.S. Department of Labor, *National Report*, September 30, 1981, Table 32, Item Number 32085.

6. Ibid., Table 30, Item Number 30010.

7. *Federal Register* 45, no. 70 (April 22, 1980): 27414.

8. U.S. Department of Labor, *National Report*, Table 32.

9. Ibid., Table 30.

10. *Federal Register* 46, no. 190 (October 1, 1981): 48606–16.

11. Mildred Rein, "Social Services as a Work Strategy," *Social Service Review* 49, no. 4 (December 1975): 515–38.

12. Martha Derthick, *Uncontrollable Spending for Social Services Grants* (Washington, D.C.: The Brookings Institution, 1975).

13. Mildred Rein, "Social Services as a Work Strategy," pp. 532–34.

14. Ibid., p. 533.

15. U.S. Department of Health and Human Services, Office of Human Development Services, Office of Social Services Policy, chart derived from state Social Service Plans and quarterly Social Services Reporting Requirements, January 1981.

16. U.S. Department of Health and Human Services, Office of Human Development Services, *Annual Report to the Congress on Title XX of the Social Security Act, Fiscal Year 1979* (February 1980), p. 80.

17. U.S. Department of Health and Human Services, Office of Human Development Services, *Social Services U.S.A.*, Annual Summary (October 1977–September 1978), pp. 11–24.

18. *Findings of the 1967 AFDC Study*, Part II. "Financial Circumstances," Table 129; *1977 Recipient Characteristics Study: Aid to Families with Dependent Children*, Part 2. "Financial Circumstances of AFDC Families," Table 16.

19. Massachusetts Senator Chester G. Atkins, Chairman, Senate Committee on Ways and Means, "Work, Welfare and the State Budget," mimeographed (January 23, 1981), p. 6.

20. *1977 Recipient Characteristics Study: Aid to Families with Dependent Children*, Part I. Table 28.

21. Stephen Leeds, *Income Sources of the Welfare-Risk Population*, The City of New York Human Resources Administration, Office of Policy Research (December 1, 1973), p. 23; Philip A. AuClaire, "The Mix of Work and Welfare Among Long-Term AFDC Recipients," *Social Service Review* 53, no. 4 (December 1979): 586–605, p. 594.

22. Lee Rainwater and Martin Rein, "Sources of Family Income and the Determinants of Welfare," working paper, photocopied, Joint Center for Urban Studies of the Massachusetts Institute of Technology and Harvard University (May 1976), p. 45.

23. See Mildred Rein and Barbara Wishnov, "Patterns of Work and Welfare in AFDC," *Welfare In Review* 9, no. 6 (November–December 1971): 7–12.

24. See, for example, AuClaire "The Mix of Work and Welfare Among Long-Term AFDC Recipients" and Mildred Rein, "Determinants of the Work-Welfare Choice in AFDC," *Social Service Review* 46, no. 4 (December 1972): 539–66.

25. For example, Barbara Boland, "Participation in the Aid to Families with Dependent Children Program," *Studies in Public Welfare*, Paper No. 12, Part I, *The Family, Poverty, and Welfare Programs: Factors Influencing Family Instability*, Joint Committee Print (Washington, D.C.: Govt. Printing Office, 1973), pp. 139–56.

26. Massachusetts Department of Public Welfare, Office of Research and Planning, "A Survey of AFDC Case Openings and Closings in August and September 1977," Welfare Census Project Paper #2, mimeographed, March 1978, pp. 2, 3, and Tables I, II, III; Massachusetts Department of Public Welfare, Office of Research and Evaluation, "Portraits of Selected Subgroups of New AFDC Recipients: Spanish-Speaking, Pregnant, and Working," mimeographed, March 1979, p. 5 and Table III.

27. U.S. Department of Health, Education and Welfare, U.S. Department of Labor, *WIN: 1968–1978*, Ninth Annual Report to Congress, p. 9.

28. Bradley R. Schiller, "Welfare: Reforming Our Expectations," *The Public Interest* 62 (Winter 1981): 55–65.

29. U.S. Department of Health and Human Services, Social Security Administration, Office of Research and Statistics, *Public Assistance Statistics*, May 1981, p. 10.

30. *WIN 1968–1978*, pp. 23, 25; Richard N. White, *Assessment of a WIN Quality Training Demonstration Project*, Phase I Report: "Characteristics of Participants," Bureau of Social Science Research, April 1980: pp. 69–71.

31. Mildred Rein, *Work or Welfare* (New York: Praeger, 1974), pp. 84–100.

32. The Heritage Foundation, "The Reagan Economic Program: Selected Budget Cuts," *Backgrounder*, no. 139 (April 29, 1981): pp. 17, 18.

33. Congressional Research Service, *Welfare Reform Background Papers: Data on Current Selected Programs*, Report No. 79–83 EPW, March 23, 1979, p. 85.

34. Mildred Rein, *Work or Welfare*, pp. 84–100.

35. Steven P. Erie and Gordon M. Fisher, "Forecasting AFDC Caseload Changes in the 1980's," Office of the Assistant Secretary for Planning and Evaluation, USDHHS, mimeographed, prepared for the 21st National Workshop on Welfare Research and Statistics, Nashville, Tennessee, August 2–6, 1981. p. 11.

36. *The New York Times*, September 8, 1981: Section B, p. 15.

37. *Congressional Record* 127, no. 116, July 29, 1981, p. H5583.

38. Ibid., p. H5585.

39. *Federal Register* 46, no. 182, September 21, 1981, p. 46773.

40. Steven P. Erie and Gordon M. Fisher, "Forecasting AFDC Caseload Changes," p. 15.

41. The Commonwealth of Massachusetts, Executive Department, letter dated October 13, 1981, mimeographed, p. 4.

42. *Congressional Record*, p. H5583.

43. Ibid., p. H5584.

44. Ibid.

45. The Commonwealth of Massachusetts, p. 15.

46. *Federal Register*, April 22, 1980, p. 27415.

47. Steven P. Erie and Gordon M. Fisher, "Forecasting AFDC Caseload Changes," p. 6.

48. *Federal Register*, September 21, 1981, pp. 46752,46753.

Bibliography

Anderson-Khleif, Susan. "Ongoing Research Journal" from the Michigan Project. February–March 1976 (Mimeographed)

———. "Income Packaging and Life Style in Welfare Families." Family Policy Note 7. Joint Center for Urban Studies of MIT and Harvard University. Winter, 1978. (Mimeographed)

Appel, Gary L. *Effects of a Financial Incentive on AFDC Employment.* Minneapolis: Institute for Interdisciplinary Studies, 1972.

Appel, Gary L. and Robert E. Schlenker. "An Analysis of Michigan's Experience with Work Incentives." *Monthly Labor Review* 94, no. 9 (September 1971): 15–22.

Atkins, Chester G., Massachusetts Senator, Chairman, Senate Committee on Ways and Means. "Work, Welfare and the State Budget." January 23, 1981. (Mimeographed)

Auclaire, Phillp A. "The Mix of Work and Welfare Among Long Term AFDC Recipients." *Social Service Review* 53, no. 4 (December 1979): 586–605.

Auerbach Associates. *An Impact Evaluation of the Work Incentive Program.* Volume I. Philadelphia, 1972.

Barr, N. A. and R. E. Hall. "The Taxation of Earnings Under Public Assistance." Working Paper, Department of Economics, Massachusetts Institute of Technology, no. 85, April 1972.

Bernstein, Blanche. "Day Care." *Studies in Public Welfare.* Paper no. 8. Joint Economics Committee, U.S. Congress, 1973.

Bianchi, Suzanne M. "Racial Differences in Per Capita Income, 1960–76: The Importance of Household Size, Headship, and Labor Force Participation." *Demography* 17, no. 2 (May 1980): 129–143.

Blackwell, Gordon W. and Raymond F. Gould. *Future Citizens All.* Chicago: American Public Welfare Association, 1952.

Boland, Barbara. "Participation in the Aid to Families with Dependent Children

Program." *Studies in Public Welfare*, Paper no. 12, Joint Economic Committee, U.S. Congress, 1973.

Bradley, Buell and Associates. *Community Planning for Human Services.* New York: Columbia University Press, 1952.

Burke, Vee and Alair A. Townsend. "Public Welfare and Work Incentives: Theory and Practice." *Studies in Public Welfare.* Paper no. 14. Joint Economic Committee, U.S. Congress, 1974.

Carter, Genevieve W. "The Employment Potential of AFDC Mothers." *Welfare in Review* 6, no. 4 (July–August 1968): 1–11.

Commonwealth of Massachusetts. Department of Public Welfare. *State Letter 242,* October 1968.

———. Department of Public Welfare. *State Letter 553,* September 29, 1981.

———. Executive Department. Letter dated October 13, 1981. (Mimeographed)

Congressional Research Service. *Welfare Reform Background Papers: Data on Current Selected Programs.* Report No. 79–83 EPW. March 23, 1979.

Cox, Irene. "The Employment of Mothers as a Means of Family Support." *Welfare in Review* 8, no. 6 (November–December 1970): 9–17.

Derthick, Martha. *Uncontrollable Spending for Social Services.* Washington, D.C.: The Brookings Institution, 1975.

Economic Report of the President. Washington, D.C.: U.S. Government Printing Office, 1978.

Economic Report of the President, 1979. Washington, D.C.: U.S. Government Printing Office, 1979.

Eppley, David B. "Decline in the Number of AFDC Orphans: 1935–1966." *Welfare in Review* (September–November 1968): 1–7.

Erie, Steven P., Gordon M. Fisher, and Liz Dayan. U.S. Department of Health and Human Services. "Preliminary Findings of the AFDC Population Study." December 3, 1980. Internal memorandum.

Erie, Steven P. and Gordon M. Fisher. "Forecasting AFDC Caseload Changes in the 1980's." Office of the Assistant Secretary for Planning and Evaluation. USDHHS, prepared for the 21st National Workshop on Welfare Research and Statistics, Nashville, Tennessee, August 2–6, 1981. (Mimeographed)

Federal Register 45, no. 79 (April 22, 1980).

———— 46, no. 182 (September 21, 1981).

———— 46, no. 190 (October 1, 1981).

Franklin, David S. *A Longitudinal Study of WIN Dropouts: Program and Policy Implications.* Los Angeles: Regional Research Institute in Social Welfare, 1972.

Friedman, Barry L. and Leonard J. Hausman. *Work and Welfare Patterns in Low Income Families.* Waltham, Mass., Florence Heller School for Advanced Studies in Social Welfare. Brandeis University, January 1975.

Garfinkel, Irwin and Larry L. Orr. "Welfare Policy and the Employment Rate of AFDC Mothers." *National Tax Journal* 27 (June 1974): 275–84.

Gilbert, Charles E. "Policy-Making in Public Welfare." *Political Science Quarterly* 81 (June 1966): 196–224.

Glazer, Nathan. "The Limits of Social Policy." A Commentary Report. *Commentary*, 1971.

Gold, Stephen F. "The Failure of the Work Incentive (WIN) Program." *University of Pennsylvania Law Review* 119. Comment (January 1971): 485–501.

Goldstein, Jon H. "The Effectiveness of Manpower Training Programs: A Review of Research on the Impact on the Poor." *Studies in Public Welfare.* Paper no. 3. Joint Economic Committee, U.S. Congress. 1972.

Gordon, David. M. "Income and Welfare in New York City." *The Public Interest* 16 (Summer 1969): 64–88.

Handler, Joel F. and Ellen Jane Hollingsworth. "Work, Welfare and the Nixon Reform Proposals." *Stanford Law Review* 22, no. 5 (May 1970): 907–42.

————. *The "Deserving Poor" A Study of Welfare Administration.* Chicago: Markham, 1971.

Hannerz, Ulf. *Soulside: Inquiries into Ghetto Culture and Community.* New York: Columbia University Press, 1969.

Hausman, Leonard J. "Potential for Financial Self-Support Among AFDC and AFDC-UP Recipients." *Southern Economic Journal* 36, no. 1 (July 1969): 60–66.

Havermann, Joel. "Welfare Report Impasse over Social Services Regulations Appears Broken." *National Journal Reports.* December 7, 1974.

Heffernan, W. Joseph. "Variations in Negative Tax Rates in Current Public Assistance Programs: An Example of Administrative Discretion." Institute for Research on Poverty Discussion Papers no. 107–71. Madison: University of Wisconsin, 1972.

The Heritage Foundation. "The Reagan Economic Program: Selected Budget Cuts." *Backgrounder* no. 139 (April 29, 1981): 1–20.

Jencks, Christopher. "Alternatives to Welfare." *Working Papers for a New Society* no. 4, Winter 1974.

Kasten, Richard A. and John E. Todd. "Transfer Recipients and the Poor During the 1970s." Paper prepared for the Second Research Conference of the Association of Public Policy Analysis and Management. October 24 and 25, 1980.

Leeds, Stephen. *Income Sources of the Welfare-Risk Population.* The City of New York Human Resources Administration. Office of Policy Research. December 1, 1973.

Levitan, Sar A., Martin Rein, and David Marwick. *Work and Welfare Go Together.* Baltimore: Johns Hopkins University Press, 1972.

Long, Russel B. *The Welfare Mess: A Scandal of Illegitimacy and Desertion.* U.S. Senate, Committee on Finance. December 14, 1971.

Lurie, Irene. "An Economic Evaluation of Aid to Families with Dependent Children." Washington, D.C.: The Brookings Institution, 1968. (Mimeographed)

———. "Legislative, Administrative, and Judicial Changes in the AFDC Program, 1967–71." *Studies in Public Welfare* Paper no. 5. Joint Economic Committee U.S. Congress, 1973.

———. "Estimates of Tax Rates in the AFDC Program." Institute for Research on Poverty Discussion Papers no. 165–73. Madison: University of Wisconsin, 1973.

Massachusetts Department of Public Welfare. Office of Research and Planning. "A Survey of AFDC Case Openings and Closings in August and September 1977." Welfare Census Project Paper no. 2, March 1978. (Mimeographed)

———. Office of Research and Evaluation. "Portraits of Selected Subgroups of New AFDC Recipients: Spanish-Speaking, Pregnant, and Working." March 1979. (Mimeographed)

Mayer, Anna and Marguerite Rosenthal. "The Poor Get Poorer: Making the Family Impossible." In *What Nixon is Doing to Us.* Edited by Alan Gartner, Colin Greer, and Frank Reissman. New York: Harper and Row, 1973.

The New York Times. December 15, 1971.

———. October 9, 1972.

———. September 8, 1981.

Piore, Michael J. "Income Maintenance and Labor Market Entry: The FAP Proposal and the AFDC Experience." *Poverty and Human Resources Abstracts* 5 (May–June 1970): 13–23.

Piven, Frances Fox and Richard C. Cloward. *Regulating the Poor: The Functions of Public Welfare.* New York: Pantheon, 1971.

Policy Implications of Alternative Child Care Funding Mechanisms. Executive Summary. Washington, D.C.: REAP Associates, June 1977.

Rainwater, Lee. *Behind Ghetto Walls.* Chicago: Aldine, 1970.

Rainwater, Lee and Martin Rein. "Sources of Family Income and the Determinants of Welfare." Joint Center for Urban Studies of MIT and Harvard University. May 1976. (Mimeographed)

Reid, William J. and Audrey D. Smith. "AFDC Mothers View the Work Incentive Program." *Social Service Review* 46, no. 3 (September 1972): 347–61.

Rein, Martin. "The Welfare Crisis." In *Inequality and Justice.* Edited by Lee Rainwater. Chicago: Aldine, 1974.

Rein, Martin and Lee Rainwater. "Patterns of Welfare Use." *Social Service Review* 52, no. 4 (December 1978): 511–34.

Rein, Mildred. "Determinants of the Work-Welfare Choice in AFDC." *Social Service Review* 46, no. 4 (December 1972): 539–66.

———. *Work or Welfare.* New York: Praeger, 1974.

———. "Social Services as a Work Strategy." *Social Service Review* 49, no. 4 (December 1975): 515–38.

Rein, Mildred and Barbara Wishnov. "Patterns of Work and Welfare in AFDC." *Welfare in Review* 9, no. 6 (November–December 1971): 7–12.

Sandell, Steven H. "Family Income in the 70s: the Demographics of Black-White Differences." October 1980. (Mimeographed)

Schiller, Bradley R. "Welfare: Reforming Our Expectations." *The Public Interest* 62 (Winter 1981): 55–65.

Schorr, Alvin. "Problems in the ADC Program." *Social Work* 5, no. 2 (April 1960): 3–15.

Schultze, Charles, Edward R. Fried, Alice M. Rivlin, and Nancy H. Teeters. *Setting National Priorities, the 1973 Budget.* Washington, D.C. The Brookings Institution. 1972.

Smith, Audrey D., Anne E. Fortune and William J. Reid. "WIN, Work, and Welfare." *Social Service Review* 49 no. 3 (September 1975): 396–404.

Smith, Vernon K. and Ayden Ulusan. *The Employment of AFDC Recipients in Michigan.* Michigan Department of Social Services. 1972.

Social Security Disability Amendments of 1980. Public Law 92-265. Section 401. "Amendments on the Social Security Act."

Stack, Carol B. *All Our Kin.* New York: Harper and Row, 1974.

U.S. Bureau of the Census. *Low Income Areas in Large Cities.* U.S. Census of the Population 1970 (PC92).

U.S. Congress. House Committee on Ways and Means. *Social Security Amendments of 1967.* 90th Congress 1st session 1967. House Report on H.R. 12080.

———. Senate Committee on Finance. *Hearings Before the Subcommittee on Public Assistance.* 95th Congress 2nd session November 15, 16, and 17, 1978. Washington, D.C.: U.S. Government Printing Office, 1978.

———. Senate Committee on Finance. *Hearings on Regulations of the Department of Health, Education and Welfare Concerning Social Services Funded Under the Social Security Act.* 93rd congress 1st session, 1973.

U.S. Department of Health and Human Services. Office of Human Development Services. Washington: Office of the Secretary, 1980. *Annual Report to the Congress of Title XX of the Social Security Act Fiscal Year 1979.*

———. Office of Human Development Services. Office of Social Services Policy, chart derived from State Social Services: Social Service Plans and quarterly Social Services Reporting Requirements. January 1981.

———. Office of Human Development Services. *Social Services U.S.A.* Annual Summary. October 1977–September 1978.

———. Social Security Administration. Office of Research and Statistics. *Aid to Families with Dependent Children: 1977 Recipient Characteristics Study.* SSA Publication No. 13-11729. September 1980.

———. Social Security Administration. Office of Research and Statistics. *Public Assistance Statistics. May 1981.*

———. Social Security Administration. *Public Assistance Statistics. December 1980.*

U.S. Department of Health, Education and Welfare. Social and Rehabilitation Service. National Center for Social Statistics. *AFDC: Selected Statistical Data on Families Aided and Program Operations.* June 1971.

U.S. Department of Health, Education and Welfare. Social Security Administration. Office of Research and Statistics. *Aid to Families With Dependent Children: 1975 Recipient Characteristics Study.* HEW Publication No. (SSA) 77-11777. September 1977.

———. *Applications and Case Dispositions for Public Assistance.* ORS Report A-12 July–September 1977, July–September 1978, July–September 1979.

———. *Assessments Completed and Referrals to Manpower Agencies by Welfare Agencies Under Work Incentive Program for AFDC Recipients.* Washington, D.C. 1972.

———. Welfare Administration. Division of Program Statistics and Analysis. *Characteristics of Families Receiving Aid to Families With Dependent Children, November–December 1961.* April 1963.

———. *Effects of the Earnings Exemption Provision Upon the Work Response of AFDC Recipients.* (Executive Summary) prepared by National Analysis, Inc.

———. Social and Rehabilitation Service. National Center for Social Statistics. *Findings of the 1967 AFDC Study: Data by State and Census Divisioin.* NCSS Report AFDC-3 (67), July 1970.

———. Social and Rehabilitation Service. National Center for Social Statistics. *Findings of the 1969 AFDC Study: Data by Census Division and Selected States.* NCSS Report AFDC-3 (69), December 1970.

———. Social and Rehabilitation Service. National Center for Social Statistics. *Findings of the 1971 AFDC Study.* HEW Publication No. (SRS) 72-03756. NCSS Report AFDC-1 (71), December 1971.

———. Social and Rehabilitation Service. National Center for Social Statistics. *Findings of the 1973 AFDC Study.* HEW Publication No. (SRS) 74-03764. NCSS Report AFDC-1 (73), June 1974.

————. U.S. Department of Labor. National Coordination Committee Work Incentive Program. Memorandum from Merwyn S. Hans. November 26, 1980.

————. U.S. Department of Labor. National Coordination Committee Work Incentive Program. Letter and Charts: "Grants to States and Program Direction and Evaluation." March 26, 1981.

————. *Public Assistance 1962.* Washington, D.C. 1962.

————. Social and Rehabilitation Service. *Reasons for Discontinuing Money Payments to Public Assistance Cases.* NCSS Reports A-11, A-12.

U.S. Department of Health, Education and Welfare. *Reports on the Implementation and Results of the 1962 Service Admendments to the Public Assistance Titles.* Washington, D.C., 1964.

————. Social Security Administration. *Social Security Bulletin* 39, no. 1 January 1976.

————. Social Security Administration. *Social Security Bulletin.* Annual Statistical Supplement 1977–79, December 1980.

————. Social Security Administration. *Social Security Bulletin* 44, no. 12 December 1981.

————. Office of Human Development Services. *Social Services, U.S.A. Annual Summary.* October 1976–September 1977.

————. Social and Rehabilitation Service. *Trend Report: Graphic Presentation of Public Assistance and Related Data 1969.* 1971.

————. Social and Rehabilitation Service. *Work Incentive Program December 1974.* 1975.

————. U.S. Department of Labor. *WIN: 1968–1978,* Ninth Annual Report to Congress.

U.S. Department of Labor. Employment and Training Administration. Employment Security Automated Report System (ESARS). (Unpublished)

————. Employment and Training Administration. *National Report.* September 30, 1980 and September 30, 1981.

————. Employment and Training Administration. "Selecting WIN Activity by Characteristics of Registrants." *National Report.* September 30, 1980.

————. Manpower Administration. *Evaluation of Supportive Services Provided for Participants of Manpower Programs.* Prepared by Camil Associates. Philadelphia, 1972.

————. *Manpower Report of the President.* 1973.

————. and U.S. Department of Health, Education and Welfare. *Manpower Report of the President.* 1974.

————. and U.S. Department of Health, Education and Welfare. *Manpower Report of the President.* 1975.

————. and U.S. Department of Health, Education and Welfare. *Reports on the Work Incentive Program.* Washington, D.C. 1970.

U.S. Department of Labor. *A Retrospective Case Review of WIN-II Completed Job Entries: Grant Reductions, Services, and Welfare Savings.* Prepared by Camil Associates. Philadelphia. 1974.

————. Office of the Secretary. *WIN: 10th Annual Report to Congress.* December 19, 1980.

————. "WIN Program: Management Information Reports." September 30, 1981. (unpublished)

U.S. General Accounting Office. *Problems in Accomplishing Objectives of the Work Incentive Program.* 1971.

————. *Some Problems in Contracting for Federally-Assisted Child Care Services.* Report to the Congress. June 1973.

U.S. Office of Economic Opportunity. *Day Care Survey 1970.* Prepared by the Westinghouse Learning Corporation. Westat Research Incorporated. Washington, D.C.: WLC-Westat Research, Inc. 1971.

U.S. Office of Management and Budget. "Federal Income Security Programs." from *Special Analyses, Budget of the U.S. Government Fiscal Year 1973.* January 1972.

————. *Major Themes and Additional Budget Details.* FY 1983.

U.S. Senate. *Congressional Record.* December 14, 1971. October 3, 1974. July 29, 1981.

————. Hearings. Committee on Finance. *Establishing Priorities Among Programs Aiding the Poor.* 92nd Congress. 2nd session. 1972.

Valentine, Charles A. "Blackson: Progress Report on a Community Study in Urban Afro-America." February 1970. (Mimeographed)

White, Richard N. *Assessment of a WIN Quality Training Demonstration Project.* Phase I Report: "Characteristics of Participants." Bureau of Social Science Research. April 1980.

Wishnov, Barbara. *Can State Government Gain Control?* Boston: Massachusetts Taxpayers Foundation. January 1980.

Index

————. Manpower Administration. *Evaluation of Supportive Services Provided for Participants of Manpower Programs.* Prepared by Camil Associates. Philadelphia, 1972.

————. *Manpower Report of the President.* 1973.

————. and U.S. Department of Health, Education and Welfare. *Manpower Report of the President.* 1974.

————. and U.S. Department of Health, Education and Welfare. *Manpower Report of the President.* 1975.

————. and U.S. Department of Health, Education and Welfare. *Reports on the Work Incentive Program.* Washington, D.C. 1970.

U.S. Department of Labor. *A Retrospective Case Review of WIN-II Completed Job Entries: Grant Reductions, Services, and Welfare Savings.* Prepared by Camil Associates. Philadelphia. 1974.

————. Office of the Secretary. *WIN: 10th Annual Report to Congress.* December 19, 1980.

————. "WIN Program: Management Information Reports." September 30, 1981. (unpublished)

U.S. General Accounting Office. *Problems in Accomplishing Objectives of the Work Incentive Program.* 1971.

————. *Some Problems in Contracting for Federally-Assisted Child Care Services.* Report to the Congress. June 1973.

U.S. Office of Economic Opportunity. *Day Care Survey 1970.* Prepared by the Westinghouse Learning Corporation. Westat Research Incorporated. Washington, D.C.: WLC-Westat Research, Inc. 1971.

U.S. Office of Management and Budget. "Federal Income Security Programs." from *Special Analyses, Budget of the U.S. Government Fiscal Year 1973.* January 1972.

————. *Major Themes and Additional Budget Details.* FY 1983.

U.S. Senate. *Congressional Record.* December 14, 1971. October 3, 1974. July 29, 1981.

————. Hearings. Committee on Finance. *Establishing Priorities Among Programs Aiding the Poor.* 92nd Congress. 2nd session. 1972.

Valentine, Charles A. "Blackson: Progress Report on a Community Study in Urban Afro-America." February 1970. (Mimeographed)

White, Richard N. *Assessment of a WIN Quality Training Demonstration Project.* Phase I Report: "Characteristics of Participants." Bureau of Social Science Research. April 1980.

Wishnov, Barbara. *Can State Government Gain Control?* Boston: Massachusetts Taxpayers Foundation. January 1980.

Index

About the Author

Mildred Rein has recently acquired her Ph.D. degree from the Heller School for Advanced Studies in Social Welfare at Brandeis University.

She has published extensively in the field of public welfare, her first book being *Work or Welfare: Factors in the Choice for AFDC Mothers* (Praeger, 1974). In addition, several of her articles in this subject area have appeared in the *Social Service Review, Sociology and Social Research*, and other professional journals.

Dr. Rein has a B.A. from Brooklyn College and an M.S.W. from Boston University.